Environmental Policies for Cities in the 1990s

ORGANISATION FOR ECONOMIC CO-OPERATION AND DEVELOPMENT

Pursuant to article 1 of the Convention signed in Paris on 14th December 1960, and which came into force on 30th September 1961, the Organisation for Economic Co-operation and Development (OECD) shall promote policies designed:

- to achieve the highest sustainable economic growth and employment and a rising standard of living in Member countries, while maintaining financial stability, and thus to contribute to the development of the world economy;
- to contribute to sound economic expansion in Member as well as non-member countries in the process of economic development; and
- to contribute to the expansion of world trade on a multilateral, non-discriminatory basis in accordance with international obligations.

The original Member countries of the OECD are Austria, Belgium, Canada, Denmark, France, the Federal Republic of Germany, Greece, Iceland, Ireland, Italy, Luxembourg, the Netherlands, Norway, Portugal, Spain, Sweden, Switzerland, Turkey, the United Kingdom and the United States. The following countries became Members subsequently through accession at the dates indicated hereafter: Japan (28th April 1964), Finland (28th January 1969), Australia (7th June 1971) and New Zealand (29th May 1973).

The Socialist Federal Republic of Yugoslavia takes part in some of the work of the OECD (agreement of 28th October 1961).

Publié en français sous le titre:

L'ENVIRONNEMENT URBAIN:

QUELLES POLITIQUES POUR LES ANNÉES 1990?

Second Printing, 1991

This report was prepared by a Project Group established under the auspices of the OECD Group on Urban Affairs. The report* is the result of a three-year inquiry which included the analysis of twenty case studies and the organisation of a major Conference in Berlin, Germany, in January 1989.

It examines various existing urban environmental improvement policies, it proposes ways and means to improve the co-ordination of policies which have an environmental impact on cities and it describes the policy instruments which are available to national, regional and local governments. Finally, it assesses local initiatives in three main areas of concern: urban rehabilitation, urban transport and urban energy management, and it proposes policy guidelines for improvement in these three areas of concern.

The OECD Group on Urban Affairs endorsed these policy guidelines in May 1990 and the OECD Council agreed to their derestriction on 18th July 1990.

* The report was written by the OECD Urban Division with the assistance of two consultants: Mr Christopher Kilby (Planner, New Zealand) for the main report and Mr Graham Haughton (University of Leeds, United Kingdom) for the Summary.

CONTENTS

List of Insets

List of Figures and Tables

Figures

Tables

STRUCTURE OF THE REPORT

The summary together with the conclusions of the project on urban environmental policies is presented hereafter at the beginning of the report. It contains a brief description of the innovative and successful approaches which are analysed in detail in the report (especially in Chapter 4) and it provides policy guidelines for action at local, national and international levels.

Chapter 1 of the report describes the various attributes of the urban environment and provides a definition of what constitutes the "urban environment". The chapter also briefly outlines the current state of the urban environment and describes the various factors that have contributed to the existing conditions. In this respect, the aspects of changing economic structures, changing societal values, increased awareness and understanding of urban environmental problems, intervention failures, and market failures are addressed.

Chapter 2 of the report presents a policy framework for the urban environment. It discusses why urban initiatives for environmental problems are necessary and outlines present policy approaches. The chapter also discusses what future policy directions will be necessary to achieve the sustainable development of cities.

Chapter 3 of the report discusses the organisational and institutional mechanisms that are necessary to achieve successful integration with respect to policy and programme formulation and project implementation within the urban environment. The range of policy instruments that are available to decision-makers for internalising environmental costs into urban development strategies is also discussed.

Although there are a large number of urban environmental issues that are currently of concern to OECD countries, it would be too lengthy a task to tackle them all in this report. As an indication of the types of initiatives and actions being undertaken in specific areas, *Chapter 4* (the last chapter of this report) focuses on three issues: urban area rehabilitation, urban transport and urban energy, and outlines the innovative approaches and lessons to be learnt with respect to financing, short and long term impacts and political feasibility.

SUMMARY AND POLICY GUIDELINES

1. SUSTAINABLE DEVELOPMENT: A CHALLENGE FOR CITIES

Cities are dynamic economic and social entities which play a driving role in the development of regional, national and international economies. They act as centres of population, production and consumption. At their best they embody all the positive advantages of economies of proximity, scale and concentration. At their worst they can produce a high degree of environmental degradation including air, water and noise pollution, land contamination and the generation of considerable amounts of waste. These factors, taken together or in isolation, significantly diminish the quality of life for urban residents and clearly indicate that cities are not making their full potential contribution to achieving global sustainable development.

Sustainable development is defined in the "Report of the World Commission on Environment and Development" as "development that meets the needs of the present without compromising the ability of future generations to meet their own needs."

The challenge posed by this concept of necessity requires cities individually and collectively to contribute to sustainable global development. Cities must therefore always frame their short-term policies in this long-term perspective of evaluating whether and how initiatives contribute to the future development of the global environment.

Pressures on the urban environment

Evidence from all OECD countries suggests that the most pressing major environmental problems facing urban areas today are:

Air pollution

This is a particular problem in urban areas, mainly because of traffic and industry. Many national air quality standards, as well as recommended concentration limits set by the World Health Organisation (WHO), are still being exceeded in the cities of OECD countries.

Water pollution

The main uses of water are for cooling purposes in power stations, various industrial applications and domestic supply. At present, water supply operations are substantial users of both space and energy, whilst the inadequate treatment and disposal of urban waste water from domestic and industrial sources too often pose health risks to the public.

Waste from cities

As cities grow and consumption per capita increases, many urban areas are running out (or have already run out) of sites for the disposal of solid wastes. In addition, more and more communities are unwilling to tolerate the creation or extension of waste disposal sites.

Noise generation

The primary sources of noise pollution in urban areas are road traffic, neighbourhood and aircraft noise. Approximately 15 per cent of the population (or more than 100 million people) in the OECD area are exposed to potentially harmful urban noise levels. In some cases this level continues to rise, particularly as road traffic increases.

Pressure on land for urban development

The growth of urban areas has led to a significant conversion of land from agricultural to urban uses over the past few decades. In some OECD countries not only is more land being contaminated in cities and more intensively used overall, but more land is being demanded for low-density suburban expansion.

Deterioration of the quality of urban life

Large cities in particular have become more congested and more polluted, making them less attractive and less efficient for both individuals and businesses.

Degradation of urban landscapes

The city itself is in some senses a non-renewable resource. The built environment of parts of many cities constitutes irreplacable national and global treasures. Though Venice is perhaps the most extreme and most precariously balanced example of this, at a different scale every city has a mixture of built environments and related cultural heritages and traditions which if lost can never be replaced.

Urban environmental policy principles

There is now a heightened public awareness and concern about environmental and related public health issues. There is a much wider knowledge and understanding of the processes involved and the limits of environmental damage that can and should be tolerated. Moreover, the spiralling costs of tackling urban environmental degradation are being recognised, encouraging initiatives to limit its occurrence. Together these factors give policy makers a strong motive to devise new solutions. Already there are some areas of general agreement on the principles involved. These can be summarised as the *need for*:

- ***Developing long-term strategies*** for the management of the urban environment in the context of sustainable global development;
- ***Adopting a more cross-sectoral approach*** to the planning of development proposals, for instance better integration of transport and land use planning. This should draw

administrative and political forces together to work more effectively for the environment;

- ***Facilitating co-operation and co-ordination*** within the public sector, and between the public and private sectors and local communities;
- ***Enabling the producers*** of pollutants to absorb environmental and social costs through fiscal and pricing mechanisms;
- ***Setting and enforcing minimum environmental standards***, to protect the various aspects of the urban environment from individual and collective deterioration – for instance, setting maximum pollution tolerance levels and encouraging the preservation of open spaces, such as parks, in cities;
- ***Increasing the use of renewable resources*** and fostering low-waste and recycling processes;
- ***Encouraging and building on local initiatives*** and community involvement, and improving local capacities for environmental activity, particularly through the retraining of local people for local jobs.

2. INITIATIVES FOR KEY ISSUES IN THE URBAN ENVIRONMENT

Introduction

In the following sections three environmental priority themes have been isolated for more detailed discussion. ***Urban area rehabilitation*** is an important issue in all OECD Member countries, which between them have amassed a tremendous store of knowledge and expertise in tackling it. ***Urban transport*** is another priority area for many OECD countries, as the rise of private transportation in particular has contributed to accelerating conditions of congestion and pollution in many cities. ***Urban energy*** is an area in which OECD countries have less experience, but in which considerable scope for positive progress exists with a view to reducing pollution and improving standards of public health. These three themes clearly do not cover the whole range of environmental issues facing cities today. They are, nonetheless, indicative of the nature and range of some of the most important problems and solutions being identified as priority areas for urban environmental policies.

Initiatives for urban area rehabilition

Issues

The massive industrial restructuring of the 1970s and 1980s left large tracts of land abandoned, as many traditional industries left the cities. On the other hand, many growing cities have developed over the same period with low quality or insufficient infrastructure and with poor environments. With appropriate government intervention to provide a strategic development framework and fund pump-priming activities, much can be done to turn around the fortunes of these areas, to realise their latent potential in contributing to the vitality of city economies. The nature and scale of problems inevitably vary between areas, from the problems of continuous incremental deterioration in the physical and social environment to the relatively sudden, dramatic shrinkage or closure of a factory or port facility. Although urban change is always and everywhere in motion, this report is primarily concerned with situations involving large sites and a considerable legacy of physical problems left behind, with, for instance, land that is contaminated and abandoned or lacking engineering structures.

Some important common themes for the management of area rehabilitation and improvement can be identified from the diversity of problems which are covered in this section. Many OECD cities have now capitalised on the creation of new opportunities which have arisen as a result of the decline of coastal and estuarine heavy industries and related infrastructure. Initiatives have been undertaken to reverse the downward spiral of decline with new investments which help generate private investment confidence and support the forging of new roles and identities for these areas.

Innovations

Special-task agencies – taking a comprehensive area-based approach – in many cases have been initiated to expedite the processes of change, for instance in Winnipeg, Canada and Dublin, Ireland; the Urban Development Corporations in the United Kingdom are another example. Local implementation of projects, involving a range of key local actors and agencies, is also often essential. Numerous examples now exist of failed attempts by central government initiatives to impose a scheme on a local area, which did not come to life until local government was encouraged to become more involved. Although the ability to recognise and be responsive to local potential is far from a local prerogative, local involvement is often a necessary, albeit not a sufficient, condition for project success.

The creation of a strategic vision and development framework for an area has underpinned virtually all successful area initiatives, providing the necessary supportive framework to attract private investors. In addition, the legacy of substantial site-specific problems has required government financial resources to clean up an area as a pre-condition to making private investment viable. Powers over site acquisition have also often been fundamental to success, helping to overcome the problems of fragmented ownership and land sterilisation by land speculators holding on to key plots of land.

The development of a range of partnership arrangements, between the public and private sectors in particular, but also with local community organisations, has been especially important. These partnerships have helped to establish common objectives, clear divisions of responsibilities and overall co-ordination in task achievement. Recognition of ***the importance of inter-relationships between economic, social and environmental objectives in rejuvenating an area*** has also been important. The creation of a high quality local environment with a high amenity value has been essential to attracting commercial developments and housing alike. Similarly, the development of an appropriate mix of housing and community facilities has often been essential in creating a new positive image for an area and minimising the dangers of social polarisation and the "leakage" of the benefits of economic upturn. And, in many instances, for instance in Vancouver, Canada, and Salford, United Kingdom, the ***successes of area schemes have had significant positive spillover effects*** in helping revitalise surrounding areas.

Policy guidelines

1. ***Strategic vision and a development framework*** are essential ingredients to a co-ordinated approach to area renewal, maximising the synergies between different schemes and reducing unproductive disturbance to existing activities;
2. ***Urban area rehabilitation has to be multi-dimensional in approach***, encompassing enhancements to the physical environment, the built environment and the social fabric, with a view to improving the quality of life for residents and efficiency of businesses. It is important that the identity of an area be enhanced, not destroyed, and especially in terms of cultural heritage and preservation of the positive aspects of existing built and natural environments;
3. ***Public-private partnerships*** can enhance the effectiveness of the activities of all concerned and create a sense of mutual trust and mutual purpose with which to propel change in a beneficial direction;
4. ***Special purpose, locally-based agencies*** are often best suited to implementing and co-ordinating urban area redevelopment, if they are unencumbered by excessive bureaucratic constraints and are locally sensitive and flexible in approach;
5. ***Urban area improvement schemes should minimise the possible negative social implications of change*** such as the displacement of former urban residents (and, in particular, the poor, the aged, the minorities);
6. ***Local initiative should be fully utilised*** in area improvement and local needs acknowledged; community participation in the process of change can be as important as the final stage of rehabilitation, improving the sense of community responsibility.

Initiatives for better urban transport

Issues

The seemingly inexorable rise of private transport has brought with it a mixture of benefits and costs for society as a whole. Nowhere is this more clear than in large cities and conurbations, many of which are now experiencing major problems of congestion, pollution, pressure on land and increasing problems of access to urban services for those without cars. In addition to these local manifestations, there are other important issues: rising consumption of a dominant non-renewable resource, oil; land pressures outside the city for better inter-urban roads; and pollution on such a scale that it is suspected of being a major contributor to global warming.

At the present time, traffic congestion is creating unprecedented inefficiency in both the functioning of cities and the use of fuel. Cities whose roads are congested day after day slow down the movement of both people and goods. In the process, slow-moving traffic increases the fuel consumption of cars and lorries, further increasing both energy consumption and pollution. Undoubtedly the scale of this problem is now threatening the economic vitality of some cities and placing unacceptable burdens on general public health. In many cities the usual response is to react to an immediate crisis by accommodating existing demands and building more roads. All too often, this short-term remedy carries with it long-term problems. Demand management which seeks to reduce demand, without overlooking it altogether, is needed with strategies ranging from greater investment in public transport to encouraging home-working.

There is a pressing need for greater co-ordination of urban transport policies, co-ordination between public and private transport modes, as well as co-ordination between transport and other policies and activities. In too many cities there is a counter-productive fragmentation of both planning and implementation powers. In particular, there is a need to plan public and private transport provision in parallel, which in many instances will require initiatives which harness the demand for private transport whilst optimising levels of accessibility within and between cities.

There remains a strong case for better internalising the social and environmental costs of urban transport into the pricing mechanism for fiscal measures. Measures which tax usage (e.g. fuel taxes) rather than ownership (e.g. taxes on sale, annual taxes) are especially efficient.

In addition, both central and local government can play leading roles in initiatives to promote public transport in particular, to manage all urban traffic in a more co-ordinated fashion and to develop and use cleaner fuels. There is significant scope to involve the private sector in these initiatives, to provide public transport facilities, to improve the design of private transport and, possibly, even to lead or participate in road pricing schemes.

Innovations

Innovation in the field of urban transport has often concentrated on management and fiscal arrangements in the short-term and on the introduction of new technologies for the longer term. The option of introducing ***road pricing*** has long been advocated but it is still rarely implemented: an area licensing scheme has been in use for 15 years in Singapore and it is proposed that such a scheme be implemented in the near future in Stockholm.

Differential vehicle taxation in Germany has recently helped promote a shift to low emission cars and certain cities, in the same country, favour the use of so-called "friendly vehicles" (quieter and cleaner than the norm) in their most sensitive areas. More generally, a number of OECD governments have introduced price differentials through their taxation measures which favour unleaded over leaded petrol.

Integrated packages of traffic measures geared to local needs and potentials have now been drawn up in some cities. In Italy for instance, traffic measures are now drawn together to rationalise the use of existing roads and parking areas, to speed up both public and private transport systems, to integrate public and private transport networks and to protect the environment in particular areas and zones. In Athens, integrated measures are being introduced to create new outer ring roads, to build new public transport networks, to co-ordinate better the different modes of public transport, restrict inner area traffic and relocate large public and private enterprises with high traffic demands to sites outside the city centre.

Local schemes, in circumstances of severe environmental conditions (e.g. smog), have recently restricted, in several cities, the use of individual motor vehicles, depending on their contribution to urban pollution.

Policy guidelines

1. ***There is a need for strategic planning in the management of urban transport systems***, moving towards long-term time horizons and away from ad hoc, incremental responses to demand. This will need to be linked to a strategic vision of future settlement patterns both within and outside particular urban areas.

Therefore, ***transport planning and land use planning*** need to be seen as inextricably linked;

2. ***Demand for private transport is growing rapidly, but cities will not cope unless some transfer is made to mass transit media***, as well as to alternative means of transport and communications, such as walking, cycling and greater use of telecommunications. Demand management in urban transport needs to do more than simply meet every expressed demand with new infrastructure, especially roads; instead it must anticipate and re-orient demand with a view to creating a locally appropriate mixture of public and private transport;
3. ***Greater co-ordination is required between public and private transport*** (e.g. through creating a separate joint administrative agency to manage urban transport in totality). This is important as it needs to be recognised that greater co-ordination is required between public and private transport;
4. ***The full social and environmental costs of urban transport need to be appreciated and absorbed by users***, as was recently agreed by European Transport Ministers*. This requires the creation of new accounting mechanisms, which should include the costs of accidents, congestion, pollution, noise and use of public space in the total costs of private vehicle and public transport use. Such new accounting mechanisms would form the basis for improving both the price structure and the provision of transport infrastructure;
5. ***The burden of transport taxation needs to be shifted further towards usage rather than ownership***, implying a move from vehicle and annual road taxes to, for instance, fuel taxes, road pricing and area licensing arrangements, in order that transport users acknowledge and pay for the urban environmental costs which they generate as a result of the frequency and extension of their transport habits;
6. ***Identifying more environmentally-acceptable ways of catering for transport demands can be considerably expedited by encouraging private sector initiative***. In particular private sector resources should be directed to both improving public transport systems and to finding less environmentally-degrading means of catering for private transport demands.

Initiatives for greater urban energy efficiency

Issues

Cities inevitably involve the consumption and, to a varying extent, production of energy for residential and commercial use. In this section we are concerned with energy provision direct to homes and business premises.

Taken both together and in isolation, the generation, distribution and utilisation of energy can all be improved to enhance overall energy efficiency and more specifically to reduce undesirable emissions. This makes sense locally, nationally and globally, since most energy production at present involves the unsustainable use of non-renewable natural resources. It is important in this context to recognise that it is not only non-renewable

* European Ministers of Transport members of the European Conference of Ministers of Transport (ECMT) met on 22 November 1989 for a special session on Transport and the Environment. The press communiqué of that session states that "determined action will be taken nationally and internationally to take a sound economic approach which takes proper account of environment".

natural resources such as fossil fuels which are involved in the production and consumption of energy. A more holistic approach would recognise that energy production and consumption are intrinsically linked to the use of, and pollution of, air, water and land, and to risks of major accidents. All these factors need to be included in a comprehensive notion of "energy efficiency" and accounted for in devising new environmentally sensitive energy policies.

For cities themselves, the advantages of a more efficient energy sector centre on creating a more attractive, less polluted urban environment. In addition, "energy efficiency" will provide cities with a further competitive advantage, particularly if energy prices rise due to environmental concerns.

As urban energy production and consumption inevitably create a range of impacts beyond the immediate boundaries of individual urban areas, better energy management is very much a matter for national and local governments to tackle together, with international action also vital to success. For national government, the need is to introduce appropriate fiscal and regulative measures to ensure that the full environmental costs of energy production are internalised into the pricing mechanism and that common environmental standards are adhered to. Since the use of "oil equivalents" as an indicator of energy efficiency alone does not recognise broader environmental resource costs, such as air pollution, a new accounting mechanism is required. Internalising social costs of resultant environmental degradation in energy production will give efficient resource users the full comparative advantage they economically deserve.

Innovations

The emergence of least-cost utility planning in the Unites States may be an important step forward, as it formally treats energy conservation as a priority alternative to providing new production capacity. Least-cost utility planning calls for systematically exploiting all economically reasonable opportunities for reducing energy demand before expanding energy supply. In this way greater co-ordination between producers to use existing capacity better is encouraged. Already, new plant building has been forestalled using this tool.

Both in terms of production and usage, locally sensitive energy schemes may improve national energy policies. Local powers in the energy field vary enormously between OECD countries, not least because energy utilities such as electricity and gas vary in the nature of their ownership, from private to national or local government, often with a combination of these ownership forms. It is difficult therefore to generalise on appropriate local initiatives, particularly in terms of energy production. This said, a comprehensive strategic framework for energy production and distribution can help foster co-ordination between energy providers, to minimise excess capacity, to facilitate an optimum location of production facilities, and to encourage maximum sharing of overhead costs. An awareness of local issues is essential to this, ranging from the nature of the local economy to local microclimates.

Energy conservation and harnessing energy demand are also important means of reducing energy demands. Many cities have played a particularly central role in encouraging, demanding and facilitating energy conservation amongst users. This is especially true in terms of improving domestic and industrial insulation, where considerable scope for energy savings often remains. In Sweden and Denmark, for instance, "local energy advisors" support investment decisions of home owners and entrepreneurs in terms of energy efficiency, and when selling a house an "energy balance sheet" is compulsory to assess its energy efficiency. Many countries have building codes which impose minimum standards for new construction in terms of insulation or take into account aspects of energy efficiency in local planning.

Combined Heat and Power Plants (CHPs) have been successfully introduced at the neighbourhood level (e.g. Denmark and Finland). Such innovative activities in the urban energy sector have contributed considerably in recent years to reducing emissions from electricity generation. The advantage of this system is that much of the heat commonly lost in energy production is actually recycled and put to use locally, whilst energy losses in transmission are reduced as a result of the proximity of supplier and users.

Off-peak sharing has been another interesting institutional arrangement for enabling electricity producers to use existing capacities more efficiently. Such measures are especially promising in areas with differing seasonal demand peaks.

Through performance contracting, private energy consultancy companies in the United States have initiated additional investment activities to restructure industrial production in more energy-efficient ways. With such schemes energy saving investments are financed and carried out for private firms as well as for public authorities, repaid on the basis of additional revenues generated through reduced energy consumption. There is an important underlying issue here, namely the need to harness the innovative potential of the private sector in developing greater energy efficiency. Central government can also do much to direct energy research towards improving technologies for utilising renewable energy sources, such as wind, solar and tidal energy.

Policy guidelines

1. ***A strategic local and global perspective needs to underpin urban energy policies.*** Awareness of, and sensitivity to, the global impacts of local policies is essential to avoid "high chimney" strategies. The production and consumption of energy for urban areas can have important spillover impacts outside individual urban areas. This requires that urban energy policies are adopted which do not involve a blinkered local perspective;
2. ***Local level co-ordination and joint responsibility*** are required between local and national government agencies. Such an approach should seek to construct urban energy policies which maximise the use of local knowledge and local conditions through a strategic local co-ordinating framework. A strong supportive national framework is essential, but so too is the need for policies which are flexibly devised, interpreted and implemented at the level of the individual urban area;
3. ***Public-private partnerships involving an enhanced role for the private sector*** are important in identifying new ways of improving energy efficiency and new organisational ways of making such advances accessible to more businesses, as for example with performance contracting;
4. ***New accounting procedures*** are required which seek to internalise in the pricing mechanism not just the energy resource but also the impacts of using other natural resources, in particular air, water and land, plus the risk of major accidents. This requires a more comprehensive definition of "energy efficiency";
5. ***Exemplary practices adopted by local government can set the lead in urban energy management***, for instance through improving the energy efficiency of public housing stock and municipal buildings;
6. ***Energy conservation in homes and workplaces needs to be more comprehensively addressed***, for instance restructuring production to improve energy efficiency, higher insulation standards and energy audits on all sales of housing;

7. ***Vulnerable social groups need to be catered for when advocating higher energy prices to encourage environmental efficiency.*** General income subsidies should as far as necessary enable vulnerable groups of the population to adjust to higher energy prices.

3. FUTURE DIRECTIONS

With the urban environment so high on the policy agenda for the 1990s in many OECD countries it is timely to establish new policy guidelines within which urban policy makers can frame programmes and design specific projects. The broad themes and guidelines which have been discussed here need to be further elaborated. In particular more international comparative evaluations need to be undertaken to:

- Assess and elaborate in detail the concept of urban and global sustainable development from the experience of individual urban areas;
- Identify and disseminate information on exemplary initiatives which help provide a sustainable urban environment; and
- Examine ways of improving co-operative arrangements between local authorities, the private sector and individuals with a view to developing cities along lines which contribute to sustainable global development.

Chapter 1

THE NATURE OF THE CHALLENGE

This chapter describes various key attributes of the urban environment and provides a definition of what constitutes the "urban environment" for the purposes of this project. The chapter also briefly outlines the current state of the urban environment and describes the various factors that have contributed to existing conditions (more detailed information can be found in "Urban Statistics in OECD Countries" [OECD, 1988] and in "OECD Environmental Data Compendium" [1989]). Related developments are addressed, such as changing economic structures; changing societal values; increased understanding and awareness of urban environmental problems; and intervention and market failures.

1. INTRODUCTION

OECD Member countries recognise that in the long run market economies can only successfully operate when social considerations are taken into account.

A similar level of consensus, however, has not yet been fully achieved on the integration of environmental considerations into the market economy. An integrated environmental approach, however, would:

- Reduce the risk of economic drawbacks in each Member country from forms of environmental degradation which transgress national boundaries;
- Bring about a better allocation of resources worldwide;
- Set the basis for long term economic growth without the permanent threat of radical disruptions caused by potential environmental catastrophies.

This report deals with both the built environment and the ecological conditions of policy to improve the urban environment of cities. It focuses upon new approaches which emphasize co-ordination between sectoral policies and the integration of environmental considerations in urban planning and management. Such approaches are regarded as necessary and integral aspects of creating sustainable economic growth. The project focuses upon:

- Improving the information on the state of the urban environment and monitoring the environmental impacts of alternative policies;
- Co-ordinating urban environmental improvements (co-operation between authorities, e.g. the establishment of an intersectoral administrative committee;

involvement of community, voluntary and private sector groups) and assessment of their impact upon different social groups and actors; and
- Integrating economic instruments into urban environmental improvement policies (internalising measurable external effects, e.g. through local taxes and pollution charges); budgeting and financing urban environmental activities; linking urban environmental improvements with urban economic development goals.

Practical examples of innovative policies, programmes and instruments to deal with urban environmental improvements are cited and a number of the more interesting approaches are described in detail in "box studies".

2. THE URBAN ENVIRONMENT – A DEFINITION

Defining the urban environment is a complex challenge. Cities are dynamic entities and their composite environments and the quality afforded by them are not only determined by the fulfilment of the material economic needs of their citizens, but also by the social and environmental conditions which prevail. These social qualities include aspects such as the healthiness, attractiveness, and safety of urban areas. Cities, therefore, have many attributes that contribute in different ways to creating these desired qualities. For example:

- The level of pollution: air and water quality, noise levels, waste disposal;
- The type of land use: the pattern of built and open land, the mix of uses, the extent of land vacancy and dereliction;
- The building stock and infrastructure: its fitness for purpose, condition, the processes of renewal and conservation; and
- The type of townscape: the design of buildings and public spaces, landscaping, traffic management, litter and vandalism.

The definition of what constitutes the urban environment can be and is interpreted in a number of ways. The narrowest interpretation is one that is concerned primarily with the appearance of urban places and embraces building design, conservation, townscape, planning. A wider definition extends this to traffic safety, the condition of buildings and infrastructure. A yet wider definition is concerned with the sustainability of urban environments and embraces resource consumption. Sustainability or sustainable development is defined by the Brundtland Commission as the ability of humanity "to ensure that it meets the needs of the present without compromising the ability of future generations to meet their own needs". The concept of sustainable development implies limits – not absolute limits but limitations imposed by the present state of technology and social organisation on environmental resources and by the ability of the biosphere to absorb the effects of human activities. Sustainable urban environments, therefore, are those which develop and grow in harmony with the changing productive potential of local, national and global ecosystems.

Recognising that ecological and built systems are intricately linked, the urban environment is defined, for the purpose of this report, as "including such physical elements as water and air quality, waste disposal, noise levels, neighbourhood conditions and availability of open and green space. It also includes ecological conditions, opportunities for recreational activities, aesthetic quality of architecture and landscape, and urban amenities (defined as characteristics and qualities which contribute to the pleasantness, harmony and cultural quality of the surroundings)".

3. THE DEVELOPMENT OF CITIES – ECONOMIC SPECIALISATION

Cities have always played and will continue to play a major role in the development of national and international economies. In OECD countries with their high levels of urbanisation, cities represent the major concentrations of investment in infrastructure, buildings and social, cultural and educational facilities. Indeed they provide the location of both production and consumption in most developed economies. Hence the efficiency with which cities provide for economic activities will inevitably influence the efficiency of the economy as a whole.

Today, more than 70 per cent of the population of OECD countries live in urban areas. Cities have evolved into complex economic and social structures due to the very large numbers of people who live, work and take their recreation in urban areas and the diversity of economic activity which has been generated by the benefits of the "agglomeration economies" afforded by cities.

Cities, therefore, have been and still are the centres of specialisation and communication, and so logically remain the motors of technological and economic progress. Specialisation was the driving force behind the technological and economic progress achieved in the past. For some time this development seemed to be sustainable and to an extent harmonious with the natural habitat. However, as part of the industrial revolution, specialised mass production and economic growth have been creating a much larger scale of problems. Large cities all over the world may be seen as a threat to the environment because of the large supply streams they are creating. Cities may also be seen as a threat to sustainable global development in that they produce huge amounts of non-recyclable waste and pollution which must be absorbed back into the ecosystem, causing problems which range from local to global in scale. The environmental problems being generated by cities are, therefore, substantial, and increasing.

On the other side, cities play a driving role in the development of regional, national and international economies. They embody all the positive advantages of economies of proximity, scale and agglomeration and they play a key role in driving technological change. Therefore, if sensitively developed and maintained, cities and towns constitute opportunities for tackling environmental problems.

4. CURRENT PROBLEMS IN THE URBAN ENVIRONMENT

Environmental conditions, especially in urban areas are a source of critical concern to OECD societies, since urban populations are particularly exposed to the combined effects of air and water pollution, problems of waste disposal and derelict land, noise and congestion. Furthermore these problems, which are worsening in many cities, are often accompanied by a lack of open space and greenery and, in certain cases, a decay of the built environment.

These problems associated with the urban environment are not restricted to any particular city size, age, or type; nor are they specific to cities of a particular OECD country. The available evidence strongly suggests that urban environmental problems exist in all OECD countries, although they are cause for variable degrees of concern, from acute and immediate to minor and local.

Water pollution

The OECD 1985 State of the Environment Report notes that surface and groundwaters have gained considerably in importance over the last few decades. In many OECD countries, improvements in both the oxygen content and in microbiological quality have occurred in some major surface waters. However, increased levels of nitrates, heavy metals and organic pollutants may have harmful consequences for the aquatic environment and pose considerable risks to public health. In addition, groundwater of good quality is becoming a scarce commodity, owing to increasing demand above the rate of replenishment and to the pollution of existing supplies.

In cities, rates of water extraction and water pollution are a primary concern. OECD statistics show that in 1985 the major uses of water withdrawal were for electrical cooling, industry and public water supply (Table 1).

The present urban water management system requires a great deal of space and energy for both supply and removal. Water pollution in combination with a too rapid rate of water extraction can cause serious harm to hydrological systems. In the United States, for example, the maintenance of adequate water supplies to urban areas in the western states and some of the major population centres of the northeastern states is emerging as a major issue, with rationing and curtailment of non-essential water use implemented in many of these areas during hot dry summers.

In urban areas both groundwater and river systems have deteriorated in quality for both human consumption and industrial needs. Pollution of water systems has been caused mainly by industrial activities, particular heavy industry, and waste disposal activities. In many countries, every major urban area has a river flowing through it, whilst some have additional extensive canal systems. In the past both have commonly been polluted by industrial and municipal sewage disposal sources. Today great improvements have been made but not uniformly. For example, in the United Kingdom, the River Thames is considered the cleanest metropolitan estuary in the world, with over 100 fish species present. However, other rivers, in the northwestern part of the country, e.g. the Irwell and Mersey, are some of the most polluted.

Air pollution

Air is a vital natural resource and needs to be managed as such because of its environmental, economic and social importance. The quality of ambient air has an impact on a variety of economically important processes. Unhealthy air can reduce human production potential and it can reduce plant productivity. In the United States, between 40 million and 75 million people live in areas that fail to meet air quality standards for ozone (O_3), carbon monoxide (CO) and particulates. In OECD countries, trends in emissions of sulphur-dioxide (SO_2), suspended particulate matter and lead have generally been downward since the mid-1970s. For example, during 1974-84 there were decreases of 58 per cent

Table 1

TOTAL WATER WITHDRAWAL BY MAJOR USES[a]

Selected countries, 1985

	Total		Public Water Supply	Irrigation	Industry (No Cooling)	Electrical Cooling
	Millions m^3	Per Capita (m^3/cap.)				
Canada	41 470	1 635	11.1	7.1	9.5	38.1
United States[d]	467 000	1 952	10.8	40.5	7.4	38.8
New Zealand[e,f]	1 900	579	27.8	..	..	..
Austria	2 120	280	24.8	2.6	23.6	47.2
Denmark	1 462	286	43.1	..	..	..
Finland	4 000	816	10.2	0.5	37.5	3.5
France[g,h,i]	39 995	725	14.8	10.5	12.0	47.3
Germany[b]	41 216	675	12.4	0.5	5.8	62.0
Luxembourg	67	183	..	..	..	..
Netherlands[c]	14 471	999	7.7	..	1.8	63.5
Norway	2 235	538	29.3	3.1	25.1	..
Spain[i]	45 250	1 175	11.8	65.0	23.2	..
Sweden	2 888	346	33.7	2.1	41.7[b]	0.3[b]
Switzerland[k]	709	109	..	..	..	..
Turkey[h,i]	19 400	389	19.1	66.0	14.9	..
United Kingdom[h,i,j]	11 511	231	..	0.7	12.4	34.0

a) Withdrawal from the four sectors do not necessarily add up to 100%, since "other agricultural uses than irrigation", "industrial cooling" and "other uses" are not covered in this table.
b) 1983 data.
c) 1986 data.
d) Secretariat estimates.
e) Industry except cooling: ground water withdrawal only. Electrical cooling: surface water withdrawal only.
f) Electrical cooling includes all industrial cooling.
g) 1984 data.
h) Irrigation: total agricultural water withdrawal.
i) Industry includes industrial cooling.
j) England and Wales only.
k) Withdrawal of lake and spring water only.
Source: OECD.

in Sweden, 39 per cent in France, 19 per cent in the Netherlands and 18 per cent in the United States (WHO/UNEP). However, national air quality standards as well as recommended concentration limits set by the World Health Organisation (WHO) are still exceeded in certain densely populated or industrial areas, especially for CO and nitrous oxides (NO_x). This is of particular concern as the health and environmental impacts of NO_x, generated primarily by road traffic, may be greater than initially anticipated. For example, upward trends of nitrogen dioxide (NO_2) levels have been found in London, Frankfort, Amsterdam, Stockholm and New York. In addition, although national CO levels are falling, measurements in Toronto, Chicago, New York, Los Angeles and Paris all showed average emissions exceeding the WHO 8 hour guideline limit of 10 mg/m^3 (Figure 1).

In addition, the control of fine particulate matter has not yet been satisfactorily accomplished and urban photochemical smog is emerging as a large scale problem. For example, in Western Europe and North America, smoke emissions from diesel engines, except in the United States, are generally not regulated and can account for 70 per cent of

Figure 1. **SUMMARY OF THE MAXIMUM 8-HOURLY CO CONCENTRATIONS IN CITIES, 1980-84**

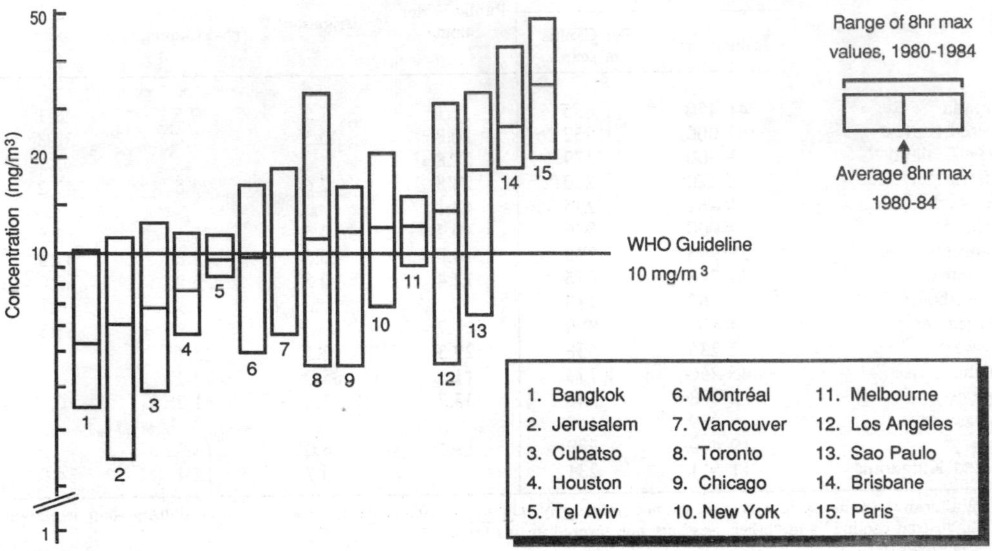

Note: The horizontal line represents the WHO 8-hr guideline value (Logarithmic scale).

Source: WHO.

smoke emissions in urban areas. There are also a substantial number of cities where the number of "high pollution days" exceeds the WHO guideline of a maximum of seven days per year. For example, between 1980 and 1985, New York, Glasgow, Madrid, Montreal, Frankfort, Athens and Brussels all exceeded the 150 ug/m³ guideline for SO_2 on 9 to 40 days each year.

Noise pollution

Increasing levels of noise within urban areas are also causing concern. Surveys and opinion polls in many OECD countries have found that the disturbance most frequently cited by respondents is noise in the home. The prime offending source of noise in terms of the number of people disturbed is road traffic, followed by neighbourhood and aircraft noise. It has been found that 5-30 per cent of the population, according to country, is regularly exposed to a noise level from traffic of over 65 dBA (Table 2). Approximately 110 million people are exposed to road traffic noise levels in excess of 65 dBA in OECD countries.

Table 2

PERCENTAGES OF POPULATIONS EXPOSED TO TRANSPORT NOISE

Early 1980s

	Road traffic noise			Aircraft noise		
	Outdoor sound level in Leq (dBA)					
	<55	55 to 65	>65	<55	55 to 65	>65
USA	63.0%	30.0%	7.0%	91.0%	7.0%	2.0%
Japan	20.0%	49.0%	31.0%	97.5%	2.5%	0.5%
OECD Europe[a]	53.0%	34.0%	12.5%	97.0%	3.0%	0.3%

a) Road traffic noise: estimates based on 12 countries; Aircraft noise: estimates for 34 airports.
Source: OECD.

In Norway, for example, for every tenth urban inhabitant the disamenity caused by noise exposure is so serious as to have an adverse effect on health. About a quarter of the residents are troubled by dirt and smell from road traffic, and almost half live in areas where the noise level exceeds 55 dBA. Ten per cent of the urban population live in areas where the level of noise is so high as to affect their health (disturbs sleep and causes stress). In Sweden, 40 per cent of urban residents, or 2.5 million people are exposed to noise levels higher than the standards which are regarded as being acceptable.

In France, it is estimated that failing the strengthening of noise abatement policies, there is likely to be a 15 per cent growth in urban populations subjected to levels of more than 65 dBA and a 40 per cent growth in populations subjected to levels of more than 55 dBA in the year 2000. The number of noise "black spots" (above 65 dBA) would increase sharply and there would be a considerable extension of areas suffering moderate noise impacts.

In the United States the proportion of the population exposed to levels in excess of 55 dBA will be 28 per cent higher in 1990 than in 1980, whilst the proportion exposed to levels in excess of 75 dBA will be 50 per cent higher. These increases will result principally from increases in the volume of traffic and urban development.

Waste

Trends in waste generation are strongly related to changes in the level and structure of consumption and production which occur in urban areas. The wastes generated in OECD countries have greatly increased in volume and changed in composition, particularly in densely populated and industrialised areas. Available data suggests that household refuse accounts for 80 per cent of municipal waste in OECD countries. Quantities of household waste grew between 1-5 per cent per year between 1975 and 1980.

Much has been achieved in OECD countries in the waste management area but liquid and solid waste management, particularly of hazardous wastes, are a concern in many cities. It is estimated that OECD countries generate about 300 million tonnes of hazardous wastes, including 267 million tonnes reported by the United States, 7 to 8 million tonnes from Pacific countries and 20 to 24 million tonnes from Europe. Urgent action is needed to reduce the amount and increase the recycling of hazardous waste and to ensure the proper disposal of future waste. For example, Spain, Germany, the United States and Turkey are experiencing problems of municipal waste management. Urban areas are running out or have run out of land disposal sites for solid wastes. Furthermore, high capital costs, public opposition to site selection and uncertainties concerning risks associated with emissions make incineration alternatives difficult to implement. To deal with solid wastes, waste reduction and recycling initiatives will have to become major strategies in many cities.

Land use

Land is a key natural resource with important ecological, economic and aesthetic functions. Ecologically, land is a medium like air or water that plays a role in many natural cycles and provides the support for natural habitats. Economically, land is a major factor input for the growing of food and fibres for human consumption and for the location and development of human activities. Land also acts as a receptor for industrial, energy and municipal wastes. Aesthetically, the importance of land stems from the value people attach to their living environment and to natural and wild areas. Land use has important impacts on environmental quality, as the location of economic activities clearly has an impact on the location of pollutants discharged or wastes disposed of, as well as on natural resource consumption by economic activities. In addition, land use is related to the functioning of ecosystems directly and indirectly impacting on ecological cycles and wildlife habitats.

The growth of urban areas and inter-urban infrastructures has led to a significant conversion of land from agricultural to urban uses in OECD countries over the past few decades. Most of the time these conversions are irreversible. Over the period 1970 to 1980, following two decades of rapid urban growth, between 1-3 per cent of agricultural land was converted to urban use.

Pressure on land is a major problem in many urban areas. In the United Kingdom, for example, although about 50 per cent of the demand for urban development is now met by recycled urban land, in some localities where development demand is strong, pressures to extend urban areas into open rural land are still great. They may become greater in the future in view of the productivity successes in agriculture which may reduce the demand for agricultural land. Within urban areas the intensification of land uses, particularly for office and residential uses, is increasingly evident. In the United States, urbanisation continues at a significant pace. Urban expansion is mainly within suburban areas surrounding large urban centres – a trend that continues long-standing U.S. development patterns of urban sprawl with relatively low population densities and a continuation of lengthy home-to-work commuting. In Germany, 10.8 per cent of land surface area was covered by buildings, industrial plants and traffic and transport facilities in 1981, representing a 36 per cent increase in coverage from 1963.

A substantial physical, social, economic and environmental deterioration of inner city areas is also a major phenomenon in many OECD countries, especially the older industrial cities in Canada, the United States, the United Kingdom, Germany and the Netherlands. In Canada this process led to:

- A substantial erosion of the population bases of Canadian inner cities. Between 1961 and 1976 the average inner city population loss was something in the order of 21 per cent, while suburban populations increased by over 15 per cent in the 1971-76 period alone;
- This loss of population caused a significant undermining of the municipal tax base;

- Problems were further compounded by the structure of local government itself. Central cities frequently belonged to different taxing and policy making jurisdictions, so that suburbanites were in essence using but not paying for many of the physical and social services provided by inner city authorities. The ability of inner city authorities to pay for services to their own resident populations was already constrained enough without adding the burden of suburban commuters.

In addition, land contamination in urban areas is increasingly becoming a problem. In the Netherlands, of the total number of projected new dwellings in existing urban areas, 30-40 per cent could not be realised as scheduled in 1986 and 1987 as a result of the land having been contaminated by previous industrial activities.

Architecture

The design of buildings in their urban settings has latterly become the subject of active public debate. In particular there is evidence of a desire to recover the richness of some pre-20th century urban environments with smaller, more human, user-friendly townscapes, a quality lost to a great extent in much of the comprehensive renewal of urban areas undertaken after World War II. This is a particular concern in the United Kingdom and in Belgium.

The preservation and renewal of "historical" cities or parts of cities is also of particular concern in countries such as Italy, Belgium and Spain.

Traffic congestion and accidents

Apart from the increased pollution emissions generated by higher uses of private transport there are increased rates of traffic congestion and accidents in urban areas. The risk of traffic accidents is high in many places. In the largest urban areas of Norway, for example, seven persons out of every 100 000 die yearly in traffic accidents, and 300 persons per 100 000 are reported injured.

Traffic congestion is an increasing characteristic of many urban areas and especially the major cities of OECD countries. In the United Kingdom, as elsewhere, average urban traffic speeds in London have remained around 30 km per hour for the last two decades. Half of all road traffic movements in the United Kingdom occur in urban areas and urban traffic continues to grow in volume at about 1 per cent a year, despite investment in public transport and in motorways and other roads bypassing towns.

A number of environmental indicators exist to evaluate the current state of the urban environment but much more research is needed to define and develop a complete set of indicators which would be useful for local, national and international decision-makers in assessing more accurately the state of the environment.

5. THE NATURE OF CHANGE: FACTORS CONTRIBUTING TO THE CURRENT STATE AND AWARENESS OF THE URBAN ENVIRONMENT

The changing state of the urban environment and the increasing awareness of environmental issues can be attributed to a number of factors. The acknowledgement of changing economic structures, changing societal values, and knowledge of environmental limits and chemical properties and pathways in many OECD countries has caused a growing public awareness and concern about the current state of the urban environment. However, these very factors, along with market and intervention failures, have contributed to the current problems of the urban environment. In spite of constant changes in economic, social and scientific conditions, environmental problems continue to be generated in urban societies. Although these factors are addressed individually below, it is recognised that they are interwoven and interdependent in their impacts on the urban environment.

Structural and locational change in the economy

Structural change in the economic development of cities is primarily the result of changing economic conditions and institutional responses. Traditional economic activities, such as the development of heavy industry, are in decline in many cities and countries, together with their associated infrastructure and services. It is this decline that has caused many of the problems of inner city decay in the older industrial cities of the United Kingdom, Canada, and the Netherlands. For example, in Canada, the major inner city areas requiring environmental and economic renewal are the legacy of old industrial sites located around waterways (a traditional transport and waste disposal medium) and large scale railway lands which, because of technological, economic and operational imperatives, are no longer a viable proposition in their downtown locations (for more details see "Managing Urban Change", OECD, 1983).

In other countries, the recent industrialisation of their economies has led to the rapid urbanisation of their populations. For example, in Turkey and Spain, these combined processes have contributed to inefficient water supply and sewerage systems, lack of green areas, and difficulties related to the preservation of natural and cultural values, particularly in large cities.

Structural change also causes locational change. At present, in highly urbanised societies, cities are subjected to suburbanisation and decentralisation (although there are now some signs of a reverse in that trend in some countries) as residents and firms seek less congested and better quality environments. For example, in the past three decades, a dominant trend in Canadian cities was a pronounced outward movement of both people and private sector capital to suburbia. In addition, the expansion of a number of Canadian central business districts provided further impetus to the suburbanisation process by displacing significant numbers of inner city residents. What caused these trends is still a matter of some dispute. Some part of the explanation probably lies in the shift in productive technology which took place at around this time leading to pressures to increase the land output ratio at a time when urban space was scarce, especially large sites for redevelopment. This caused established firms seeking more space to leave urban areas, and new firms to favour locating at more spacious green-field sites.

Within industry itself there is the growth of newer "high technology" activities which have different locational requirements compared to those of traditional industry. The growth in importance of service activities and "high technology" industry and their requirement for high quality environments, often motivated by the need to retain skilled staff, is leading to development pressures on regions and cities which are perceived to offer high quality environments. These are rarely the older industrial areas. Whilst the initial decline in economic performance of the largest urban areas in particular may have been the result of changing economic conditions, it is clear that the general environment in the older cities made them less attractive places in which to locate and that subsequent in situ industrial decline worsened this situation. Essentially, a process of negative "cumulative causation" set in.

Similar pressures are felt in tourist areas. For example, in Spain tourist-led growth has been another triggering factor of an accelerated urban development process, especially in the localities along the Mediterranean coast, which redirected their economic activity towards real estate construction as a way of immediately accumulating wealth. This excessive construction has been to the detriment both of the natural and built environment and the cultural heritage.

Changing societal values

The change in pace of economic development in cities has been paralleled by a shift in societal values and attitude. This shift has led to a greater general demand for a better quality of life, interest in cultural and ecological heritages as a part of leisure activity, and a better quality environment. The parallel economic prosperity of OECD countries has meant that people have sought greater access to recreational and leisure opportunities close to urban areas and also have a desire for increased mobility through automobile use.

In many ways society has conflicting values which require resolution: for example, a desire for private car use but also for less air pollution and congestion. Higher aspirations and income levels have led to a greater number of automobiles and the associated increase in traffic problems in all OECD societies. In the majority of OECD countries the social and wealth connotations associated with car ownership makes it politically difficult to implement strict pollution abatement policies with respect to automobile use.

In addition, greater leisure hours have contributed to an increased demand for clean harbours and waterways for recreational rather than industrial and transport activities and the creation of more greenfield areas for leisure activities. This has been a particular concern for the Vienna region in Austria, and Oslo in Norway.

Changing societal trends have also caused a reversal of attitude towards the desirability of living in inner city environments in many cities. For example, in Canada, after three decades of inner city decay, inner city environments have been rejuvenated due to, amongst other things:

- A sharp increase in the fashionableness of "downtown" and inner city living;
- A greater incidence of childless couples, with no need for those suburban amenities traditionally focused on the needs of children;
- An increase in marital breakups, with the resultant increase in "singles" for whom proximity to work and recreation downtown no longer needed to be counterbalanced by the consideration of the needs of children;
- A greater number of two-career couples with the financial resources to afford the high costs of "downtown" housing;
- A greater societal concern about the incursion of new suburban development on viable agricultural land;

– A much greater public appreciation of the aesthetic and architectural value of historic buildings, the vast majority of which were located in "downtown" areas.

Increased knowledge

Thanks to increased knowledge of the extent and effects of pollution and an improved understanding of pollutant transport pathways and of the critical role of the environment for ensuring world sustainability, past practices once accepted are now known to be primary causes of many of today's environmental problems. For example, in the Netherlands, the knowledge of the extent and nature of soil pollution in urban areas has grown in recent years. Since the establishment of a legal framework including standards for chemical composition of the soil, estimates of the extent of the sanitation task have repeatedly been adjusted. A recent survey has found that in 1986, 20 per cent of all planned housing construction (percentage relates to the number of housing units) in the four largest municipalities was located on sites where soil pollution required sanitation measures.

Market and intervention failures

Broadly, market failures occur when, for any one of several reasons, the market is distorted and private efficiency is not maximised. The market fails to account for the costs of environmental pollution because these costs are external to the short-term profit maximisation objectives of some entrepreneurs. Internalisation of these costs into a market framework is therefore a prime objective for policy. Market failures embrace, for instance, the conventional environmental questions of appropriate effluent levels, noise controls, safety considerations, and aesthetics. In urban economies to date, the internalisation of environmental costs into the market has generally been partial and ineffective. In the past this failure has mainly been due to a lack of knowledge of the nature of environmental damage and the type of market policy necessary to internalise relevant costs. In more recent times, however, it is more a reflection of a hesitation on the part of governments to fully implement polluter-pays and user-pays mechanisms, which would better internalise environmental costs into the market system.

Government intervention failures occur when, for a variety of reasons, there is interference with the private optimum, usually by government, to achieve other policy objectives. This interference can impose costs which are not adequately considered in the decision-making process. In the urban context, intervention failures often stem from governments' primary concern with short-term policies such as employment creation, the attraction of industry, income distribution, provision of public services and migration. Environmental considerations are not top priorities in these instances. Urban authorities and governments are primarily concerned with the economic and social conditions in the areas under their jurisdiction. As a result there is an inevitable tendency for competition to develop to attract employment, production, income, and investment. Whilst in many cases this may pose no environmental problem, in some instances, particularly where there are economies of scale in production, it may be of "strategic interest" for an urban authority to offer inducements to attract specific types of industry or encourage certain types of economic development. In the short term, this may be particularly intrusive on the urban environment, apart from the long-term implications (such as dereliction, waste disposal and water pollution) to which short-term policies can contribute. Intervention failures can, therefore, have short-term implications through direct policy impact and long-term implications by setting in place undesirable future framework conditions.

Intervention failures, therefore, stem from the nature of the intervention rather from the fact that government intervention is, per se, inappropriate or wrong. Official policies in many countries aimed at easing congestion (in the widest sense), whilst not initiating the problems, probably added to the decline and resultant imbalances in many urban economies. Policies such as suburbanisation and transportation contributed to the decay of inner city areas, increased automobile use and the decline of public transport systems.

For example, in the Netherlands, many neighbourhoods were built without provision for links to railway services. Public transport was not provided until there was sufficient demand for it, to avoid losses during the initial period of operation. The new town of Zoetermeer (satellite of The Hague), for example, did not qualify for a railway connection until there were 50 000 inhabitants; by then people had become accustomed to travelling by car. Cars demanded the adaptation of the residential environment. Parking facilities had to be extended and road safety deteriotated while fumes, noise and lead levels increased. In Sweden, the rapid rise of automobile use in the Stockholm area is also partly attributable to policies which encouraged the suburbanisation of Stockholm County and taxation and financing policies which promoted automobile use.

In Canada, decentralisation away from inner cities was also encouraged by housing policies of the day, which encouraged single-family home ownership by increasing the volume and the availability of mortgage funds and through direct financial incentives. Local governments also accelerated the suburbanisation process, through both their own capital spending programmes and planning regulations which encouraged low-density, land consumptive development patterns.

The majority of urban environmental problems have, therefore, been caused by the inability of the market to fully internalise the environmental costs of the successful economic specialisation of cities and the failure of governments to rectify this situation and to take account of the urban impacts of different sectoral policies. The missing link which could have made cities even more successful and less environmentally degrading was feedback as to the extent to which sectoral growth contributed to or detracted from a healthy and balanced development of the system as a whole. Many systems within cities, for example urban transport and waste, could well be considered "unhealthy systems" for the welfare of the city.

This chapter has shown that a wide variety of problems exist within the context of the urban environment. To overcome these failures and effectively solve these problems, an effective policy framework for the urban environment is necessary. The next chapter outlines present policy approaches to the urban environment and discusses future policy directions to achieve the sustainable development of cities.

Chapter 2

A POLICY FRAMEWORK FOR THE URBAN ENVIRONMENT

1. IS URBAN ENVIRONMENTAL POLICY NECESSARY?

As cities grow in size and political importance, urban environmental problems and opportunities can be expected to assume an even higher priority on the public policy agenda than they do today.

For example, with respect to community expectations, a recent survey on the urban environment in Spain, revealed that:

- Of the people interviewed, 77 per cent think that it is possible to reconcile the conservation of the environment with economic development; and
- Likewise, 62 per cent are of the opinion that priority should be given to environmental protection, even at the risk of curtailing economic growth.

In the United States, a summary of polls by the Roper Organisation and Time/Yankelovich found that the percentage of respondents who felt that environmental regulations "have not gone far enough" rose from 30 per cent to 45 per cent during the period between 1980 and 1985, while those who felt that regulations "have gone too far" declined from 25 per cent to 15 per cent during the same period. Similar trends were found for measures that required polluters to pay for damages or clean-up and in favour of increased regulatory enforcement.

It is an integral part of the ideological and political culture in the majority of OECD countries to accept and even expect that it should be the public sector which is the initial driving force behind efforts to protect and improve the urban environment. The rationale for public investment in urban environmental improvement is in part that the process of urban change has left a legacy of environmental problems that discourage private investment. Arguably the cost of private sector redevelopment may eventually fall to such a level that the conditions for private investment will re-emerge. In the meantime, the public costs of a poor environment and sub-optimal provision and use of infrastructure are unacceptable. As a result, it is generally accepted that the public sector can and must play the initial catalytic role in major urban interventions and it is seen as perfectly legitimate for public imperatives to override private property rights, where the latter must be sacrificed for the greater public good. Importantly, however, it has been shown that with initial public sector investment, favourable rates of private sector investment follow. For example, in Canada, Vancouver's South Shore Project, with an initial investment of $20 million, stimulated private sector investment of $130 million, a leverage factor of nearly 7:1. In Barcelona, Spain, renovation projects fulfilled the desired objectives only when the public sector set the framework for private initiative.

In addition, there is an increasing emphasis on the growing responsibility to finance environmental management programmes from local revenues, which will require urban governments to accept a substantial strengthening role both in defining local and national strategies for environmental improvement, and in implementing effective, integrated, intermedia management programmes. In the United States, for example, during the 1980s, local government spending accounted for slightly less than one-half of all U.S. national resources spent on environmental management. This proportion had risen to about 55 per cent by the middle 1980s and is projected to account for about 65 per cent by the end of the century. A recent survey undertaken by the Group of Economic Experts of the OECD Environment Committee on public expenditure on pollution control (waste, water, and air) shows that in all instances, the majority of the expenditure is from local government. Of the five countries surveyed, only in Norway did central government contribute a substantial proportion of the total expenditure (Table 3).

It is clearly important to define an appropriate policy framework for the improvement of the urban environment as one element for the successful development of urban areas. Whatever the current state of an urban area, its economic performance is closely linked with environmental matters. For example, the different elements of the inner city problem are inter-connected and there is mounting evidence that improving the quality of life in cities may also draw back scarce categories of labour, stimulate the relocation of employment and produce a more diverse economic base. Such improvements are likely to make urban areas more attractive both in the sense of being more pleasant for the existing labour force and of inducing migration, especially of more highly skilled workers. On a broader geographical basis, environmental improvements in urban areas may also help to reduce pressures on land elsewhere and *ipso facto* result in wider environmental benefits being generated.

Table 3

PERCENTAGE OF PUBLIC EXPENDITURE ON POLLUTION CONTROL BY LOCAL, REGIONAL AND NATIONAL GOVERNMENTS

Type of expenditure	Level of government	US 1986	Denmark 1985	Netherlands 1985	Norway 1985	Sweden 1986
Investment	Central	0	2	–	28	18
	Regional	0	0	–	14	0
	Local	100	98	–	58	82
Running costs	Central	16	5	6	–	11
	Regional	0	2	0	–	2
	Local	84	93	94	–	87
Total	Central	10	4	–	–	14
	Regional	0	2	–	–	1
	Local	90	94	–	–	85

Notes: All percentages are based on gross public expenditure figures.
All figures are calculated from country questionnaire replies to a survey undertaken by the OECD Group of Economic Experts.

Improved environmental conditions do not, therefore, automatically prevent the achievement of other policy objectives and indeed often the reverse is true. For example, in the United Kingdom, the Association of Metropolitan Authorities (a representative body for local authorities in large cities) has declared that "environmental improvement will help to create a new economic base, both by attracting the new industries of the technological age and by creating new jobs to maintain the green fabric, provide leisure services and recreational facilities and support tourism". In Finland, the recent urban population trends clearly illustrate that those towns reputed for the quality of their internal and external environment attract most new production and immigration. Policy for local environmental improvement is, therefore, of great importance in both stimulating and supporting local economic development.

2. PRESENT POLICY AIMS AND INITIATIVES

In the current programme of country initiatives for the urban environment, specific policies are being enacted in a wide variety of areas. In fact the majority of the problems identified in the previous chapter are being tackled simultaneously by all the Member countries. However, as can be expected the nature of the policies given priority in each country is very much a reflection of the current states of growth or decline within the urban setting. In the United Kingdom, Canada and the Netherlands, the key urban priority is the regeneration and renewal of inner city areas, especially those associated with old industrial cities. In Turkey and Spain, emphasis is on the implementation of effective and efficient sewerage networks, the upgrading and removal of inadequate areas of housing and squatter settlement, and the orderly planning and siting of industrial activities. In the Scandinavian countries, whose cities are relatively new and do not suffer to the same degree from problems associated with older declining industrial cities, policies are currently being pursued in the areas of energy efficiency and environmentally-sensitive energy use, as in Finland; the improvement of the internal living environment of urban residents, especially for disadvantaged groups such as the elderly and the disabled, as in Sweden; the provision of adequate opportunity for urban residents to participate in open air recreational activity, as in Norway; and problems associated with air pollution and congestion from traffic, as in Sweden and Norway. The adequate provision of recreational opportunities is also a primary concern for urban areas in Austria. The problems associated with traffic are of primary concern in Greece and Italy. Other major policy initiatives include the greening of cities, as in Japan, and protecting the character and heritage of historical cities as in Belgium.

The current range of policies to improve the urban environment is, therefore, extensive, encompassing urban planning, housing policies, urban conservation, environmental enhancement, infrastructure provision, urban economic policies, traffic, waste management and recycling, energy management and nature conservation. For example, upgrading of an inner city residential area requires measures such as rehabilitation of housing units and their immediate neighbourhood; reducing emissions of noise and air pollution; attractive designing of public space in streets and squares; reclaiming street space for multiple purposes; improving opportunities for recreational activities; and conservation of architectural quality.

It is evident, however, that in OECD countries, there is no single public policy or programme for the improvement of the urban environment. Policies to control a variety of sectoral activities which impact upon the urban environment arc implemented as problems occur or when it is judged to be politically opportune to deal with them. These initiatives are seldom sufficiently co-ordinated, the result being that, in many instances, optimum environmental impacts are not realised and accounted for on thc local, national or international level.

The major challenge for urban environmental policy is to effectively combine the multitude of sectoral policies which impact upon the quality of life of city dwellers and the ecological balance of cities. Policy should aim to reduce local pollution and noise, provide good opportunities for open air recreation, preserve the landscape and cultural values and help to realise the goals of social development and well-being. At the same time, it is necessary to lessen the town's impact on the natural environment *inter alia* by reducing energy consumption, by reducing polluting discharges of importance in a global/national perspcctive, and by avoiding reductions in biologically important resources of land. Other areas for priority effort are renewing older parts of the towns, strengthening the identity and sense of community in local environments, and protecting thc residential and central areas of towns against through traffic.

Policy for the urban environment, therefore, needs to be refocused so that it recognises the full importance of encouraging the sustainable economic and social development of cities with respect to resource use and environmental quality. Environmental quality and the sustainable use of natural resources are increasingly being seen as a potential asset to the competitiveness (regionally, nationally and internationally) of urban locations. In particular, Norway, as a result of the Brundtland Report requires urban areas to give priority to: reducing energy consumption and discharges of importance in a global/national perspective, e.g. carbon dioxide and nitrogen oxides, and avoiding degradation of biological resources, including valuable agricultural areas and ecologically important areas. The message for cities is that they need to become more sustainable – locally, regionally, nationally and internationally.

3. THE SUSTAINABLE DEVELOPMENT OF CITIES – THE FOCUS FOR THE FUTURE

This new approach to dealing with the urban environment has particular ramifications for the way cities view the impacts of their activities and the associated adjustments necessary by national, regional and local initiatives. Policy for the urban environment in this context is not restricted to management of impacts within the local environment alone but recognises the fact that urban initiatives also, in many instances, impact upon regional, national and international environments.

Necessarily, the concern in this report is two-fold, with the sustainable development of urban areas individually, and also with the contribution of each urban area to global sustainable development. Urban areas can never be regarded as self-contained entities, as they need to interact economically, socially and environmentally with other areas as an integral dimension of their vitality and growth. The challenge is to obtain a better understanding of these relationships and, in particular, to act upon an improved knowledge of environmental interactions to foster optimum mutual economic growth and improvements in quality of life.

The role of urban areas in the processes of environmental degradation and improvement is one rife with tensions and seemingly unresolvable contradictions. Urban areas with dense concentrations are necessary in terms of economic efficiency and, in effect, work against the environmental disruption of more dispersed patterns of production and consumption, which would impact adversely on rural areas in particular. The opposite perspective would point out that urban areas concentrate environmental problems to such an extent that they damage the natural ability of damaged ecosystems to regenerate themselves. In addition, the concentration is damaging to human health and to the general quality of life of urban residents and those affected by the spill-over effects of environmental degradation.

Any policies to improve the urban environment need to be aware of such tensions and seek to promote environmental policies which result in net improvements for both the urban environment itself and the global environment.

If sustainable development is to be a useful concept, it requires careful definition. Building upon sustainability as outlined by the Bruntland Commission (Section 1.1), it is important to define what is meant by both development and sustainability. Development can perhaps be best defined as including all factors that lead to increases in societal well-being and the preservation of existing freedoms, self-esteem and self-respect. Development is, therefore, something much wider than economic growth. The term "sustainable" in this context can perhaps be best defined as a non-declining welfare or "utility" for society or perhaps as a non-declining set of development indicators over time. Therefore, if development is to be sustainable, it must encompass a full appreciation of the value of the natural and built environments in terms of their contributions both to present societal well-being and for intergenerational equity.

This means that the valuation of environmental capital must be undertaken correctly so that the full value of the services provided by it are recognised. Sustainable development will require that environmental capital does not decline over time.

To achieve greater sustainability, cities will have to strive to fulfil at least two principles of sustainable urban development:

- The principle of "functional and self-regulatory growth";
- The principle of "minimum waste".

According to the principle of functional and self-regulatory growth, economic growth in each specific sector of the economy would be valued against the net contribution it makes to the system as a whole. Feedback systems would signal where growth rates are too low or too high. In theory, market economies would be able to rely on price signals as a ubiquitous, immediate feedback system. To achieve this, prices would have to give more information than they do today.

To date there has been little achievement in including information about the depletion of environmental resources in everyday consumption and investment decisions. A number of attempts have been started, however. The United Nations is currently reviewing its system of national accounts. Through "satellite" resource accounts the depletion of the stock of national capital would be made explicit. Thus rapid rates of economic growth based on exploiting the natural resource base would be seen as what they are: signals of illusionary gains in income and permanent loss of wealth. External environmental and social effects must be internalised in prices and the systematic collection of information at the city level and redesigning urban charges and taxes under these aspects could make a major contribution. Cities should be used as "urban observatories" that systematically give early notice of specific social, environmental and economic problems before they have reached national or international dimensions.

The principle of minimum waste has its basis in the functioning of natural ecosystems which incorporate an efficient recycling mechanism of materials required for life to exist. Society's waste production has been linked to specialisation and mass production, combined with sectoral and linear thinking. Too often only a small part of a product's life cycle was considered as the responsibility of producers and as for the rest, it was vaguely felt that "nature would take care of it". This is no longer a viable option, if indeed it ever was. The necessity to minimise waste is echoed in the 1989 White Paper of the Japanese Environment Agency which states that, in addressing the challenge of building "Ecopolis", the city where humans live in harmony with the environment, it will be necessary to devise environmental policies that make the urban ecosystem "more self-reliant, stable and circulatory, in many ways similar to natural ecosystems".

Energy efficiency and conservation, together with waste disposal, treatment and recycling, are areas where further practical urban research is needed. It is already recognised that it is not sustainable to ship waste to developing countries or to dump it in the ocean, and international organisations are striving to achieve agreements on these issues. A parallel effort is also necessary at the local level if sustainability is in reality to be achieved.

There is already evidence that cities are beginning to conceive of economic development in a much broader, more holistic and more pro-active way. A number of local innovative experiments exist, which effectively implement environmental policies of national consequence at the local level. For example, in Sweden, Stockholm County has proposed a system of traffic toll fees for the achievement of national environmental objectives associated with traffic pollution in Stockholm City, which is now being evaluated by the national government for its applicability to other Swedish cities. To achieve more effective implementation, giving flexibility to local authorities provides the opportunity for innovative and cost effective approaches to be developed. Local authorities could be considered as "urban laboratories" providing information on what works at the local level and what does not. Information about successful approaches to local implementation should be collected, evaluated and disseminated as effectively as possible.

Cities have a substantial challenge to meet if the urban environment is to be managed in a sustainable way. To meet this challenge, the framework in which policies are generated and implemented is crucial. Of importance are the role of the different levels of government, the organisational and institutional mechanisms that are necessary for success, and identifying what policy instruments are available and how they are currently being used to solve problems in the urban environment. Cities can make a major contribution to solving both local and national environmental problems by focusing on integrated management approaches in their own self-interest to improve the overall health, safety and economic prosperity of their communities.

Chapter 3

ORGANISATIONAL INTEGRATION AND ECONOMICS – A KEY FOR SUCCESS

This chapter discusses the organisational and institutional mechanisms that are necessary to achieve successful integration with respect to policy and programme formulation and project implementation within the urban environment. The range of policy instruments that are available to decision-makers for internalising environmental costs into urban development strategies is also discussed.

1. DEFINING INTEGRATION

Integration will be crucial to achieve the sustainable development of the urban environment. In both the short and long term, greater integration between sectoral policies and management regimes is necessary for successful urban environmental initiatives. An integrated approach will minimise the impacts of unco-ordinated action, which in the past has contributed to many of the problems associated with the environment in urban areas. Integration will also ensure that urban-generated impacts on the national and international environment are also included in policy responses and initiatives.

Integration requires the conscious and systematic consideration of the many diverse elements of the urban environment in seeking optimal management solutions. In conceiving, designing, implementing, maintaining and terminating a policy, complementary and competing objectives must be balanced to solve and anticipate problems, mindful of intertemporal and equity implications. Integration, therefore, requires the development of policies that are preventive and anticipatory as well as reactive. Unintegrated policies are characterised by the belated recognition of the consequences for the objectives of other sectors. The most successful programmes for ameliorating problems associated with the urban environment in OECD countries have all used an integrated approach.

Integration can be achieved if a number of organisational and institutional mechanisms are consciously implemented (Figure 2). It will be necessary to establish an appropriate hierarchy of management and take integrative action at the levels of both policy and programme formulation and also at the level of project implementation. Of the mechanisms identified for the achievement of integrated environmental policy, three are perhaps critical for success: flexibility, commitment and leadership profile, and public participation.

Figure 2. **FRAMEWORK FOR INTEGRATION**

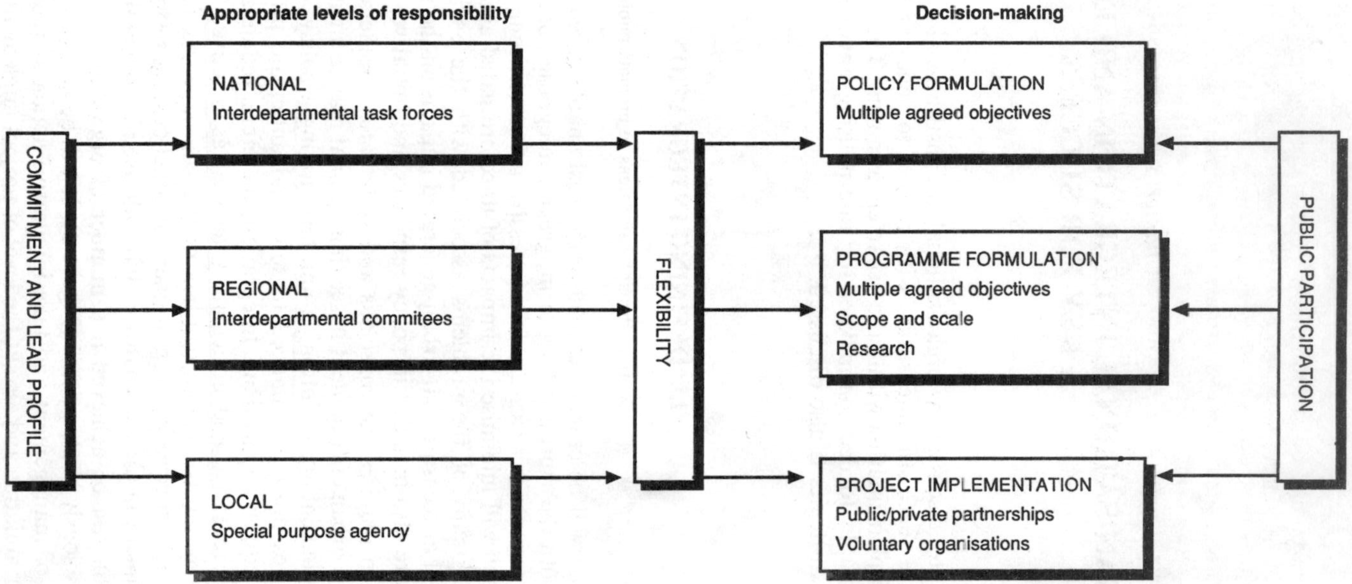

Flexibility

The achievement of sustainable development within the urban environment will require a more flexible redefinition of the conventional responsibilities and reporting relationships within and between levels of government and their administrative bodies, as well as a willingness on their part to surrender some of their former autonomy in the interests of attaining the more comprehensive objectives of integrated projects. In the Vienna-Danube project, Austria, for example, the adoption of a flexible organisational structure meant that the administrative powers available to the public authorities could be extended and supplemented as necessary and that expertise available outside the administrating authorities could also be integrated into the formal planning process. This was also one of the innovative aspects of environmental management in Angers, France (Inset 1). In general, giving greater flexibility to local authorities to deal with environmental problems provides the

Inset 1. **Integration of Environmental Policies at the City Level – The Case of Angers (Maine-et-Loire), France**

In launching protocols of agreement to take account of the environment in urban planning and administration, the French Ministry of the Environment and the Interministerial Committee for Towns (CIV) wanted to help local authorities which had in the past endeavoured to give effect to and run comprehensive local urban environment policies. Angers is covered by one of these protocols, which provides for a series of projects undertaken in accordance with a three-year plan (1986-88).

To give effect to this protocol, Angers is applying a global environmental strategy via a series of projects concerned mainly with:

- Education and public participation, through campaigns to promote public awareness;
- Control of pollution and noise, and the monitoring of complaints;
- Collection and recycling of waste;
- Cleanliness of the town;
- Creation of natural surroundings in the town.

To meet the above objectives the municipality of Angers strengthened its municipal health office by converting it into a full environment/health department in 1983. The department employs 219 people and is charged with providing logistic and technical backup for the town's environmental policy. The deputy mayor responsible for the environment is also in charge of the green and open space department which employs 124 staff and works in close liaison with the town planners prior to the launching of any major project.

To make the residents of Angers more aware of their environment, several promotion campaigns were undertaken. All of them were conducted in collaboration with environmental and district associations, by an extra-municipal board which meets from time to time in each quarter.

In addition to keeping residents informed and monitoring changes in the urban environment of Angers, it is proposed to institute an "instrument panel" for the urban environment which, in liaison with voluntary bodies, will help target action more effectively.

What is crucial is that a "consciousness of the environment" has been created:

- Among elected representatives and in the municipal administration where awareness of the environmental impact of everything the municipality does extends across the entire municipal policy field. The advice of the environment department is asked for on a very wide range of questions; and
- Among the public at large which is not only kept informed and aware but is also listened to and asked to participate.

In line with this consciousness there has been an overall strategy to back up a series of pilot projects: economic town contract, pilot town contract against noise, and more recently a protocol of agreement to take account of the urban environment.

opportunity for locally-sensitive innovative and cost-effective approaches to be developed. In this way the successful implementation of environmental policy is most likely to be achieved.

Commitment and leadership profile

Continuing commitment and the leadership profile of a key politician or high-profile administrator are necessary for the successful implementation of a policy of integrated mangement of the urban environment. Without willingness and an ongoing commitment, traditional sectoral policy approaches are likely to continue. At the local level, the successful implementation of projects requires dynamic (and persistent) leadership. In future, it is most likely to be the idiosyncrasies of time, place, and intergovernmental chemistry which will determine whether this crucial leadership comes from government, from business, from labour, or from community organisations. It is certain, however, that without determined, courageous and locally-based leadership, cities will be unable to come anywhere close to realising their full environmental and socio-economic potential. Examples abound. In Istanbul, Turkey, the commitment and leadership of the mayor were one of the major keys to the success of the Restoration of the Golden Horn. In Salford Quays, United Kingdom, commitment from the mayor and a local private developer ensured the success of the renewal project. In Angers, France, the mayor played a dominant role in implementing a comprehensive urban environmental programme.

Public Participation

Effective public participation is also necessary if policy objectives are to be fulfilled and projects successfully implemented. While it is largely corporate bodies, whether in the public, private or non-profit sector which shape the urban environment, it is predominately the individual citizen who experiences it. Effective mechanisms must be found for encouraging and integrating citizen participation in policy formulation. In Belgium, the renewal of the City of Mons is a good example of effective public participation. The preparation of an "Urban Charter" on which the future of Mons is now based would not have occurred if it had not been for the close co-operation and participation of the citizens in its formulation and implementation. In Japan, the formulation of anti-pollution agreements for Yokohama City was also greatly determined by the participation of a community organisation – "The Environment and Health Protection Council of Naka and Isogo Wards".

Enhanced consumer power can also be used for influencing the agents of environmental change. Governments should ensure that the process of agency decision-making is a public one, in so far as this aids the openness of decision-making and the process is not, therefore, confined within a single agency or group of collaborating agencies. In the United Kingdom, the Public Request to Order Disposal Scheme (PROD) enables the public to identify unused land owned by public authorities and to request that the Secretary of State for the Environment use his legal power to force the owner to put the land on the market, if the Secretary of State deems it appropriate.

2. APPROPRIATE LEVELS OF GOVERNMENT RESPONSIBILITY

With the growing number and complexity of regulations in the field of environmental policies, implementation has become a major concern of governments. In implementing policy for the urban environment it is important to consider to which part of the organisational hierarchy management issues and functions are allocated. An integrated approach does not require all of the issues and functions to be allocated to a single level of government and a single structure. Issues and functions should generally be allocated to the scale closest to the people receiving the flow of goods/or services from the management activity. Administrative responsibility for the urban environment should be pushed as far down the administrative chain and rest as close to the ultimate user groups as possible.

In the past, in dealing with problems associated with the urban environment, it was chiefly the national governments which mainly influenced, initiated, and implemented urban environmental policy initiatives. Although this is still largely true in the majority of OECD countries, there is now a greater awareness of the necessity to involve the local level in the decision-making and implementation process. In the future, local authorities will need greater autonomy to manage the diversity of urban environmental problems.

So as to better implement urban environmental policies, several countries have created greater functions and powers at the regional level and rationalised the number and boundaries of local authorities. For example, in Greece, regional environmental authorities have recently been established, local authorities amalgamated and greater consultation linkages between all government levels established. This process has meant that national policies are better fulfilled at the local level, and local authorities have a more active role in the decision-making process.

Today, therefore, local governments must be a major participant in terms of decision-making and finance, and in leading public opinion. Local governments are the governments closest to the people. Dissemination of real power was one of the more innovative but largely unnoticed dimensions of Winnipeg's Core Area Initiative, Canada. Indeed where appropriate, programmes can and should be delivered by the affected community and neighbourhood groups. Obviously regional and national governments have an important role to play; but they could have their hands less on control, and instead perform the important role of facilitation, advocacy, leadership, and performance control rather than prescription of specific approaches which might not be optimal in the local context. Ideally central government would be most effective if it deployed its human and financial resources to support and enhance a local initiative and in so doing made that initiative a locally-sensitized articulation and instrument of central policy. National governments are in the best position to monitor success and failure in local experience and to disseminate innovative approaches.

3. POLICY AND PROGRAMME FORMULATION

The achievement of integration with respect to policy and programme formulation requires the development of common policy objectives and the recognition of an appropriate programme scope and scale. These aspects are, in turn, best achieved by the formation of interdepartmental task forces, committees and boards.

Common policy objectives

Policies and progrmmes which are enacted in order to achieve more sustainable urban environments should pursue common policy objectives. These formally and explicitly recognise the inter-relationships of different sectoral policies, whose integration minimises detrimental impacts and maximises benefits of urban environmental programmes. In Canada, for example, eight recent urban redevelopment projects involving obsolete industrial and waterfront lands all shared at least five common policy objectives:

- The improvement of the urban built environment;
- The creation of fresh economic activity and vitality in the inner city through the construction of new or rehabilitated residential, retail, cultural, and office facilities;
- The creation of a larger indigenous residential population base for the downtown and inner city;
- The socio-economic stabilisation of inner-city neighbourhoods through the attraction of middle and upper income residents back to the downtown and inner city; and,
- The strengthening of the municipal property tax base.

Integrated urban environmental policy objectives are also being pursued in Norway, through "environmental packages" (integrated environmental programmes), where measures to reduce pollution from agriculture, industry, transport, the municipality and consumers are co-ordinated with and supplemented by measures to give greater opportunities for open air recreation and to improve the local environment. The Norwegian government has also established a commission for community development with a mandate to coordinate governmental policies affecting local communities and to further develop the practical possibilities of these policies using local pilot projects (Inset 2).

It is important that integrated objectives flow through policy into specific programmes. In Canada, for example, in the Winnipeg Core Area Initiative (CAI), the CAI's housing renovation programme was explicitly tied to its employment and training thrust with the result that the CAI was able to achieve no fewer than four objectives simultaneously: the construction of needed housing and community facilities at reduced cost; the provision of training and job skills for those previously unable to compete in the urban job market; the generation of income for the trainees along with the associated increase in their self esteem; and the reduction of municipal welfare costs since the trainees no longer required social assistance payments. This example neatly illustrates the principle that programme content should ideally attempt to achieve a politically sustainable balance between commercially-oriented efforts and social development objectives.

Research

Research programmes for environmentally-positive urban development should also be undertaken to find innovative and cost-effective solutions to environmental problems. Research, development and assistance programmes should also be co-ordinated in concert with local government representatives to capture and adapt for replication, innovations already defined and proven; to avoid unnecessarily redundant or duplicative development

Inset 2. **Programme for the Development of an Organisational Structure for Environmental Protection at the Municipal Level – The Case of Norway**

The World Commission for Environment and Development set the scene for a strong local involvement in environmental matters. One of its main strategies is to "Think globally and act locally". As part of this process, the Ministry of Environment and other State bodies, together with the Norwegian Association of Local Authorities (KS), started a three-year programme for the development of an organisational structure for environmental protection at the municipal level. This programme is being run in approximately 90 representative municipalities, encompassing most major cities.

The goal of the programme is to test different political and administrative organisational structures and control mechanisms, gauging their suitability for taking on the responsibility of environmental protection in the municipal decision-making process. In addition, the goal of the programme experiments with the delegation of responsibility from the Ministry of Environment to the municipalities in the area of environmental protection.

An evaluation of the programme will take place in 1991, the year of the next municipal elections. Before this time, each of the municipalities must establish a new political body to deal with environmental matters. In addition, a condition for taking part in the programme is that the municipality must have an environmental director or advisor. The Ministry of Environment is financing this new position as a part of the agreement with each of the participating municipalities.

The Ministry of Environment has recommended that the municipalities establish an independent environmental committee. This model enables the municipal authorities to create a political body which can concentrate on environmental issues, will have the necessary legal measures and authority and, at the same time, can have an overall view of environmental projects in the municipality. Although this will be the main organisational model, other alternatives will also be tried, giving responsibility either to a select interdepartmental committee; to one of the existing committees (e.g. culture, technical or health) or to the executive committee of the municipality.

The municipalities participating in the programme will work out their own environmental and natural resource programmes, which will serve as guidelines for the politicians on all the main issues of environmental protection. In addition, the Ministry of Environment together with the KS is working out an educational programme for the politicians participating in the environmental committees.

The programme is followed up by a regional forum where the municipal authorities participating in the programme, the county administration, the county council, the county branch of KS, and the regional research institutions are members. The county environmental director is chairman of this regional forum. Its main purposes are to follow up the programme in the counties, exchange information, and co-ordinate and evaluate the programme.

Interest in the development programme has been overwhelming. It is anticipated that some municipalities not participating will also change their political organisation in accordance with the objectives of the programme, independently creating a position of environmental director/adviser. The municipal authorities will be invited to participate in the regional forum in their county. The reactions to the development programme in the participating municipalities has on the whole been positive. Good results have been reached by putting more emphasis on environmental problems. In the municipalities, people have become more involved in volunteer work to clean up the environment, and the polluters have had to pay for their negligence. Many of the municipalities participating in the programme have come a long way in their work with the municipal natural resource programme.

efforts; and to assure the practical usefulness of programme results for application within urban areas. These broader initiatives must be complemented by effective procedures to support training for local staff, as well as continuing experience exchange and technology transfer among local government managers. For example, in Norway, an interdisciplinary research programme on road traffic, environment and health in urban districts has been going on since 1985 and will finish in 1989. Another interdisciplinary research project has been established for the purpose of achieving better integration of environmental considerations into physical planning. The project "Nature-positive and environmentally-positive urban development" is intended to elucidate the consequences for land use and development in towns and urban centres of following up overall superior environmental objectives.

Appropriate scope and scale

Urban initiatives should be as conceptually broad and comprehensive as can realistically be supported by the financial, organisational and political resources available. However, when formulating programmes of action it is essential to identify the most appropriate scope and scale. If the project is overly ambitious, as public consciousness and expectations have been raised up to that level, then failure to meet any of the stated objectives will cause the project to become susceptible to criticism and severely damage the project's reputation. For example, in Spain, the lack of concentration and defined scope of refurbishing projects has hindered the exemplary and driving importance that might have been achieved by the performance of the projects in a limited area. A sensible choice of area should include opportunities that can be realised quickly and at low cost as well as more complex and intractable problems. The creation of confidence is a key ingredient of success in urban improvement. For example, with respect to urban renewal initiatives, attention and effort should focus on priority areas, to reinforce and establish the identity of an area, to mobilise the support of households and businesses in the area and, thereby, maximise local environmental improvement and community pride in it. This is one of the fundamental principles behind the "small area approach" for urban renewal projects in the United Kingdom.

Interdepartmental task forces, boards, committees

To help facilitate the formulation of integrated urban environmental policy and programme initiatives, interdepartmental task forces and committees should be used to co-ordinate national initiatives, and at the regional/local level environmental boards or committees should be established. In Norway, in order to help achieve integration of environmental considerations into national policy in different fields, the government has established a special Committee on the Environment, consisting of eight Ministers of State. In addition, a development programme for environmental protection in the municipalities is intended to increase the municipalities' responsibility and improve their administrative qualifications to carry out tasks connected to the environment. In Italy a joint commission consisting of representatives from the "Ministry for Urban Areas, Regions, Provinces and Local Authorities", co-ordinates urban projects which have already been prepared or which are already under way, and which have been submitted by authorised bodies. In Japan, cities such as Yokohama have established councils to investigate and advise the mayor on important environmental issues.

Of all the OECD countries, Finland has one of the most decentralised systems of local environmental administration. Municipalities have an Environmental Protection Board entrusted with the abatement of air pollution, waste management, noise abatement, permits and notifications related to water protection, nature conservation and other environmental protection tasks. The Environmental Protection Boards are to unify environmental administration both locally and on a country-wide basis. When the administration is developed, decisions will increasingly be taken in these boards, so that official municipal bodies will be involved in matters of the urban environment.

So as to ensure that policies affecting the urban environment are implemented consistently throughout each country, the creation of local environmental boards should be embodied in legislation. In the United Kingdom, for example, there is no legal or formal obligation on district local authorities to act across the board on urban environmental issues. Some district authorities have, however, created separate "environment departments" responsible for the management of relevant services like development control, land reclamation, conservation and renewal, and traffic management. Some have undertaken environmental audits or published environmental strategies in which these and also other programmes run by other agencies are examined and given specific objectives and targets. However, overall there is relatively little formality or uniformity about the institutional arrangements within local authorities for managing the improvement of the urban environment. This is true also for Spain, where urban and environmental matters are dealt with by different offices.

4. PROJECT IMPLEMENTATION

The use of special purpose agencies, public/private co-operation and voluntary organisations are important mechanisms to ensure that integrative policy initiatives are successfully implemented.

Special purpose agency or corporation

Generally speaking projects for the urban environment should be implemented at least in part by a special purpose agency or corporation, free of the diffuse day-to-day responsibilities of the ongoing government departments. Its creation is usually imperative if the necessary level of focus and commitment is to be attained. The staff of these agencies must be highly motivated and, if they are to be truly effective, will require sufficient political and administrative credibility and support to be able to mobilise and direct governmental resources beyond those of the central agency itself.

For example, in Canada, the emergence of public sector development corporations in the mid-to-late 1970s, were designed to catalyse large scale redevelopment in urban areas where fragmented land ownership and/or a lack of private initiative and profitability had hitherto prevented it. The public corporations were either directly empowered with the legal ability to assemble land against the private owner's wishes if necessary (i.e. expropriation powers) or else they borrowed those powers from their governmental creators. These powers gave the public corporations a major advantage over their private sector counterparts, and have generally allowed them to dictate the location, pace and nature of the development if necessary. In addition to sizable land bases, the public corporations were generally well capitalised, with budgets ranging from $20M to $100M.

A similar concept is used in the United Kingdom. Urban Development Corporations (UDCs) combine a specialist agency and an urban approach. An urban development area is designated and a UDC established to regenerate it. UDCs are the agents for major environmental improvement in very rundown urban areas. In Spain, the creation of Local

Management Offices to carry out the management of urban regeneration programmes independently is supported by enabling legislation.

Public-private partnerships

With shrinking public finances and investment budgets public/private partnerships are a key to the economic success of urban environmental projects, ensuring an ongoing commitment from the private sector to the development of the urban economy. The financial participation of the private sector is becoming critical to the success of urban environment projects, as a direct concomitant of the decreasing capacity of government to carry the financial burden. The private sector must play an active and aggressive role if future projects are to reach their economic potential. While this lesson may seem self evident, it is one which will have increasing relevance in the coming years, for public sector discretionary budgets will continue to contract as deficit-containment and fiscal responsibility become an ever-greater preoccupation of public policy. Public/private partnerships need to recognise and attain the difficult balance between the imperatives of private profitability and the attainment of public policy and social objectives.

Partnerships take very many different forms ranging from relatively informal joint working arrangements to formally constituted joint ventures. They vary in the partners involved, although partners are usually drawn from the government, business and non profit-sectors. They vary also in the control over manpower and financial resources that is ceded by the partners to the partnership. Generally, government brings the start-up capital; the exclusive legal capacity to undertake large land assemblies; and the ability to supply subsidised financing, tax incentives, training programmes, and other financial inducements. Public authorities are usually responsible for the cleaning up of derelict land and obsolete structures, polluted waterways and soil, and implementing new infrastructure, green space, and environmental amenity policies. They set the authoritative overall planning context and thereby reassure each private investor that their project will fit into a general development framework which protects their investment and upon which they may rely. The private developer contributes substantial additional capital, financial expertise, and a capacity to construct, market, and manage the project which is on the whole more efficient than that of most public agencies. In Canada, while government has generally been the initial catalyst of large scale urban redevelopment, it has then tended to proceed by way of public/private sector partnerships, whereby the dominant investment by far is made by the private sector. In 1987 a total of roughly $66 billion was invested in construction in Canada, and less than 10 per cent of this figure was attributable to the public sector.

In addition, the day-to-day management of the urban environment is also increasingly being undertaken by public/private partnerships. For example, in the United Kingdom, local authorities are the main providers of parks and open spaces but work on maintenance and improvement is increasingly contracted out. Proposals have also been made to separate local authorities' public provision and regulatory roles in waste disposal. Local authorities still undertake measures to upgrade the townscape by greening and cleaning programmes (though non-profit voluntary organisations are increasingly active in this field, assisted financially by public authorities). These changes are part of the policy in the United Kingdom to transfer service provision from the public to the private sector (privatisation) or, while retaining responsibility with a public authority, to transfer to the private or voluntary sectors the delivery of the service (contracting out) (Inset 3).

Inset 3. **The Groundwork Foundation – Making Urban Environmental Improvement Happen – United Kingdom**

In the United Kingdom, the Groundwork Foundation is a fast developing network of local trusts committed to creating active working partnerships between diverse sectors of the community. Groundwork aims to tackle problems of dereliction, restore landscapes and wildlife habitats and make positive use of the wasteland in and around towns and cities.

This approach leads to the completion of complex projects which any single group acting independently would find almost impossible to undertake successfully. The key lies in harnessing the talents and resources of very different but complementary sectors of the community and uniting them in one cause – the improvement of their local environment for the benefit of all.

Private industry is involved for its advice, expertise and financial muscle; local governments contribute financial support and a sound knowledge of local conditions; central government, through the Department of the Environment, the Countryside Commission and others, helps to sustain operations with funding and grant support for projects; and voluntary and community groups join the partnership to provide the workforce needed to bring many of the projects to fruition. Groundwork Trusts act as the catalysts to identify and set up schemes; and provide a bank of environmental advice and experience.

Initially Groundwork Trusts receive up to 50 per cent of their running costs from the Department of the Environment. The Groundwork Foundation liaises with DOE officials over the areas where Trusts are to be established. The enthusiasm with which local government has greeted the Groundwork Trusts has much to do with the organisation's perpetual growing strength. Local authorities are essential partners and prime instigators in establishing Trusts and providing funding.

With the private sector, Groundwork works with companies of any size at national and local levels, from multi-nationals like IBM and Shell to small concerns like garden centres. Private sector companies help in a number of ways, including: sponsorship of a local scheme or an entire national campaign; donations of money, land, equipment, and materials; and secondment of staff with management or technical talents to benefit Groundwork-inspired projects.

Essential to any labour-intensive urban environmental regeneration project are the voluntary organisations, national and local with whom Groundwork has effective and far-reaching involvement. Groundwork works closely with the British Trust for Conservation Volunteers, the Community Service Volunteers, Tidy Britain Group, Civic Trust, Friends of the Earth and the Royal Society for Nature Conservation.

From its beginnings in North West England, in 1982, Groundwork has grown to a national network of 15 Trusts, with four to five new Trusts now being formed each year. The success of Groundwork has been well recognised in the United Kingdom and recently its activities have gained European recognition: the Foundation has won a contract to investigate the potential for forming environmental groups similar to itself in France, the Netherlands and Germany.

Voluntary organisations

Voluntary organisations, interest groups and associations are a key element of public action and programme success within the urban environment. Public support to non-governmental organisations may trigger off considerable communal effort among the members and, in this way, give good value for money invested by the authorities. Organisations in the local community can mobilise considerable local resources, particularly for improvements to the physical environment. In the United Kingdom, the voluntary environmental movement has grown in strength in recent decades and has become increasingly committed to practical action. Locally-based, non-profit, voluntary organisations are engaged in a variety of environmental improvements – energy saving, waste recycling, building rehabilitation and the greening of vacant land. While such voluntary intiatives are essentially local, there are national networks and organisations promoting and supporting action of this kind. For example, the British Trust for Conservation Volunteers organises volunteers for practical conservation projects, and Friends of the Earth nationally campaign for more sustainable cities.

In Canada, a good deal of the "consciousness" raising which produced a quantum shift in urban environmental values can be attributed to the work of Heritage Canada, a non-profit endowed trust set up by the federal government in the early 1970s. Heritage Canada's principal mandate is to promote national awareness of heritage issues, both through the dissemination of information and expertise and, to a more limited extent, through direct funding. The overwhelming focus of the foundation's activity is on advocacy, networking, information gathering and dissemination, and the supplying of expert technical advice.

In Norway, the Ministry for the Environment gives economic support to non-governmental organisations working for a better urban environment, e.g. the Royal Norwegian Society for Rural Development, a nationwide association of residents' organisations and other organisations in the local community. The Ministry co-operates with such organisations, and with research institutions to develop systems of study and co-operation aimed at making the local population better equipped to participate in municipal planning and make an effort to preserve green areas in the local environment. In Spain, local "neighbourhood organisations" have been successful in bringing together the community and city authorities to undertake successful environmental projects at the local level.

The organisational mechanisms outlined above are of considerable importance for achieving integrated action with respect to the implementation of urban environmental policy. Experience in Member countries suggests that such integrated approaches can be undertaken and are a key to success. However, of equal importance is the provision of appropriate instruments which can provide the right incentives for internalising the costs of urban environmental impacts.

5. ECONOMIC INSTRUMENTS

Traditionally, governments have tended to implement environmental policies through direct regulation, coupled with systems of monitoring and sanctioning of non-compliance ("command and control"). The most obvious advantage of direct regulation is the grip authorities have on the behaviour of actors, with a more or less certain outcome in terms of environmental effectiveness.

However, the use of economic instruments to control environmental pollution has been increasing for a number of reasons, including:

- Economic stagnation and reduced government budgets have induced an interest in more cost-effective approaches;
- Direct regulation of societal processes seemed to have reached a level of decreasing efficiency, which called for "deregulation" or regulatory reform. In fact the enforcement of regulations can be difficult and in many cases insufficient;
- Charges could be used as a source for financing environmental measures, even when principally designed for incentive purposes.

The use of economic instruments, therefore, can bring about improved cost effectiveness, provide an ongoing incentive to reduce pollution and stimulate technical change, and provide greater flexibility in enforcement and choice of pollution control measures, whilst also providing an important source of revenue to finance environmental policy.

Economic instruments, however, rarely act as substitutes for direct regulations, nor should they. The choice is rather between various combinations of direct regulation and economic instruments. In practice, pragmatic approaches to new economic instruments seem to prevail: economic instruments are adjuncts to direct regulations in mixed systems. In such combinations economic instruments raise revenues for financing environmental measures, provide incentives to better implement the associated regulation and can stimulate technical innovation. Direct regulations are maintained because of their grip on actors, provided they are enforced effectively.

The range of economic policy instruments available to tackle environmental problems in urban areas is, theoretically at least, substantial. In practice, the number of those used are comparatively limited and, in any case, the application is seldom optimal.

The discussion of economic instruments is made more complicated both by the diversity and interactive nature of environmental considerations and by the fact that most authorities introduce packages of measures with specific instruments rather imprecisely targeted. The instruments also often have diverse effects (either negative or positive side-effects) on aspects of urban activities which are of environmental concern even if they are not being directly targeted. Given the range of urban environmental problems, the interaction between the policy instruments themselves can often be substantial. In this sense, it is not really very helpful to talk of particular instruments being best suited to be targeted at a specific form of environmental problem. Further, the impact of any individual instrument, will be conditional upon other policy instruments in use, and also upon the policies being pursued, for other non-environmental reasons. For example, some countries employ waste effluent charges and noise effluent charges as revenue raising devices rather than as strict instruments of environmental improvement. On occasions these will be reinforcing effects while in others the measures will work against each other.

Rather than trying to utilise individual policy instruments, it would probably be more fruitful to consider the "portfolio" of instruments which is likely to prove most efficient at handling the adverse environmental effects encountered in an urban area at a particular time. The actual use of the various policy instruments depends very much on the general economic condition of the urban area being considered. The problem is that urban economies are dynamic entities and the importance of the various policy tools very much depends on which stage in a growth cycle the economy is going through.

Accepting these caveats about treating policy tools in isolation, the main instruments of urban environmental policy can broadly be broken down and discussed under the headings below.

Externality pricing

The essence of the policy instruments used in charging for externalities is that the full costs, including the environmental costs, of any activity are fully reflected in the prices charged. A specific externality charge would be levied for the environmental damage caused and the full opportunity cost of the scarce resource used. With such a regime in place, residents and firms in an urban area would fully appreciate the true costs of their activities and thus "consumption" of the environment would be at an optimum level. There are two main approaches to externality charging.

The Polluter-Pays-Principle

The underlying idea of the polluter-pays principle is that the costs of environmental damage are directly borne by the producer generating the pollution, noise, danger, etc. (i.e. the negative externality is directly internalised). In its broadest form this may involve the offender paying to meet emissions standards, thus raising costs of producing the polluting product. More narrowly, it would involve a direct charge, equal to the extra damage done, at the desirable level of production or activity (an "optimal externality charge"). Either way, costs and prices are increased, thus sharing the burden of paying for pollution control between consumers and polluters. The more polluting the product the more its price will signal that fact.

While the more specific form of the instrument has a very well established pedigree in economic theory the rate of adoption of pollution charges has been comparatively slow, except in the field of water pollution control. Some urban externalities have, however, been internalised in specific cities. The use of crude "road pricing", in Singapore, involving the adoption of an area licensing system, for instance, produced positive effects on the levels of traffic congestion (Table 4), noise, accidents and air pollution after its introduction in 1975.

One of the difficulties of direct externality charges is that they need to be applied across the whole range of environmental costs if they are to be fully efficient. In the context of road pricing, for instance, congestion is reduced in the area where the road price is enforced (and thus noise levels, accident rates, air pollution, etc. are reduced within that area) but this can spread traffic to other areas which may be even more environmentally sensitive. It can also lead to rapid and excessive building on areas adjacent to the road pricing area – indeed there is some evidence of this in Singapore. An effective way of overcoming these effects is to ensure that the pricing scheme being developed covers an entire urban area. This is one of the innovative aspects of a road pricing scheme being proposed for Stockholm, Sweden. In this scheme, it is proposed to implement a cordon toll

Table 4

THE SHORT TERM IMPACT OF AREA LICENSING IN SINGAPORE

Time (a.m.)	Vehicle Type	Traffic May 75	Traffic May 76
7.00-7.30	Cars	5 384	5 675 (+5.4%)
	Total vehicles	9 800	10 332 (+5.4%)
7.30-10.15 (Period of control)	Cars	42 790	10 754 (–74.9%)
	Total vehicles	74 014	37 587 (–49.2%)
10.15-10.45	Cars	n.a.	6 636 (+2.7%)
	Total vehicles	n.a.	13 805 (+2.7%)

pricing scheme around the entire urban area of Stockholm so as to reduce NO_x emissions by 30 per cent from the 1980 level by 1995.

The User-Pays-Principle

The user-pays-principle requires that the user of a resource should pay the full social cost of supplying the resource. It implies, for instance that users should pay the full cost of providing water and related services, including treatment costs. It is normally seen as a policy instrument for dealing with natural resource management. In the specific context of the urban environment, the user-pays-principle is relevant in terms of providing guidance for cost allocation and recovery at the disposal end of natural resource use (especially water).

User charges are quite widespread in their application for effluent discharges by industry and residents of urban areas. These charges are, however, generally of an "administrative" nature rather than being strictly economic in their form. They cover the costs of treatment but are not designed to reflect the full social costs of the activity generating the effluent.

User-pays and polluter-pays mechanisms should be combined and applied more widely in the context of the urban environment. The use of such mechanisms are an effective way of internalising damage costs and realising the full social costs of a particular resource use. In this way specific consumers and polluters bear the costs of their actions rather than society in general. Governments need to consider more seriously the implementation of these mechanisms, if the urban environment is to be managed on a more sustainable basis.

Taxation

A number of innovative taxation mechanisms also exist for protecting the urban environment. At present, taxation measures are generally targeted at resource ownership (e.g. building tax and car ownership tax) rather than at resource use. Taxation measures targeted at resource use would more directly recognise and account for the potential environmental damages which may be caused by such use.

Land use taxation, for example, could be an effective instrument to handle the problems of privately owned derelict land. This taxation would be on unused land and would reflect both the opportunity cost of disuse in a traditional economic sense but also embrace the external costs of its being left derelict. While it may seem that land taxation of this kind would, in fact, cause the least derelict land to be brought back into use first, because its commercial potential would imply a high rate of tax, the externality element in the opportunity cost calculation would counteract this. One would assume that once the land ceased to be derelict some other supplementary mechanism would be required to ensure that the environmental implications of the new activity were optimal. In Turkey, for example, industrial establishments have to contribute to a Pollution Prevention Fund a certain amount specified according to the harmful effects they might exert on the environment, as well as to the characteristics of the site where they are located.

Vehicle use taxation would also be an effective instrument if targeted at the air pollution, noise and congestion impacts of the urban environment. High taxation on behaviour rather than on ownership could have important implications for internalising environmental damages.

Subsidies and grants

The definition of what constitutes a subsidy can take many different forms. Because environmental costs are often largely external to the consumption and production process, it can be argued that taxpayers in general have been subsidising current production processes which generate environmental costs. In this respect, society in general is subsidising inappropriate resource use as producers and consumers pay indirectly for the environmental costs and risks they impose on society. Traditionally, however, subsidies have been defined as payments and incentives that are employed to create a financial incentive to ensure the fulfilment of an environmental policy objective due to the difficulty of internalising environmental costs into production and consumption decisions. Subsidies take the form of direct grants, tax breaks, tax incentives, etc. With respect to the urban environment, public monies may be made available either as a straightforward payment for the reduction of pollution (e.g. through tax incentives, soft loans or grants) or as a payment to support a less environmentally intrusive alternative (e.g. urban public transport subsidies to attract trip makers away from the automobile).

Direct subsidies

The number of straightforward subsidies given in developed economies for water treatment and waste disposal are substantial and much of the money is related to urban-generated effects. Countries such as the United States and Germany, in particular, give subsidies to encourage "end-of-pipe treatment". In Finland, catalytic convertors for petrol driven cars are exempt from taxes, whilst tax incentives are also given for the introduction of desulphurisation technologies in coal fired power stations. The major problem with such subsidies when employed in isolation is that they generally offer little incentive for those generating the external costs either to adopt less environmentally intrusive practices or to cut back on their primary activities. Indeed, subsidies for environmental improvement can have economically disadvantageous effects in terms of efficiency, and may even be counterproductive environmentally. For example, high subsidy shares in investment costs of pollution control facilities, as implemented in the United States waste treatment plant construction programme, induce plant operators to design capital intensive facilities with too much reserve capacity as a consequence. This leads to inefficient solutions.

Transfer inducing subsidies

Subsidies to environmentally less intrusive activities may attract users from the primary source of the problem but, unless the degree of substitutability is large, there is always the potential for the overall level of activity to rise. Public transport subsidies designed to attract urban car users from their vehicles, for example, may well simply generate more traffic in aggregate which outweighs any small reduction in automobile travel. In most OECD countries, unleaded gasoline is made the most economic fuel by tax incentives. The issue here is really an empirical one relating to the size of the cross-elasticities of demand for the goods and services in question.

Emission trading and controls

Emission controls and standards are perhaps the most widely used instrument of environmental protection. They have a long history, especially in the fields of air and water quality protection.

In terms of strict efficiency, local standards would appear preferable to the adoption of national emission standards. The latter do not guarantee that the marginal costs of environmental improvement will be equalised across all urban areas and, in consequence, the uniform standard will be too generous for some cities and too severe for others. There are also theoretical grounds for differential standards based upon enforcement and compliance costs.

One approach which has been adopted in countries such as the United States is to make emissions standards more flexible by allowing emissions trading or "bubbling". This involves the re-ordering of prescribed control limits within a single plant or group of plants – the sum of the physical emissions released remains the same. The difficulty from the urban perspective is that this allows trading between polluters on the basis of their private benefits from having additional pollution rights. Given the interaction of sources of pollution and the compounding effects when pollutants are concentrated in small areas, the eventual outcome is unlikely to produce the optimal spread of emissions. Methods of designing marketable pollution permits which avoid this problem have been proposed; if correctly employed, they could provide a tool to contain adverse environmental consequences of urban growth without seriously hindering the growth process itself.

However, with no overall national or international system of monitoring there is a tendency for intervention failures to emerge since there is an incentive for individual cities to try and attract more industry and employment by relaxing environmental controls. The Japanese system attempts to avoid this. The Basic Law for Environmental Pollution Control requires prefectural governors to develop comprehensive control programmes for areas where concentrated industrial activity and population create excessive pollution. These control programmes, though locally determined, must, however, be in harmony with applicable policies of the central government. One outcome of these programmes has been the formulation of anti-pollution agreements at the city level. These agreements are determined by negotiation between local governments, businesses and residents in order to prevent pollution of the local environment. Anti-pollution agreements make it possible to implement detailed appropriate pollution prevention and control measures that are best suited to the geographical and social conditions of each urban environment (Inset 4).

Land-use planning

Land-use planning controls can take a wide variety of forms and are generally exercised by several levels of government. At present there is insufficient co-ordination between land use planning and other sector planning. For example, neither transport planning nor energy planning is systematically integrated with land use planning. However, experience demonstrates that a more co-ordinated approach can do much to mitigate negative urban environmental effects.

For example, in Finland, energy on average amounts to 45 per cent of the total running costs for residential areas, which are thus remarkably high. Of these costs, heating takes about half and commuting nearly a quarter. Microclimate conditions may cause up to 10 per cent variations in heating energy requirements in individual buildings and 3 per cent

Inset 4. **"Anti-pollution Agreements" in Japan**

Anti-pollution agreements are a kind of contract between the local authorities, inhabitants and the business sector to reduce or prevent pollution caused by local business activities.

The first agreement of this kind was signed in 1952 between Simane Prefecture Government and two local companies to develop a waste water treatment plant; to prevent business activities until the water quality satisfied standards set by the prefecture; and to compensate for the damage caused by the waste water. This agreement was a pioneering "anti-pollution agreement".

The next major anti-pollution agreement occurred in 1964, when Yokohama City concluded an agreement with an Electric Power Company which was going to build a new power plant in the city. As a condition of selling reclaimed land to the Electric Company, the city asked this company to submit a pollution prevention plan, and imposed very stringent conditions for the installation of the plant. Since this time, as a complement to regulations, anti-pollution agreements have become a widely used tool for preventing urban environmental pollution. The use of anti-pollution agreements is widely known as the "Yokohama method".

Anti-pollution agreements were first used to fill the gaps created by the absence of adequate pollution-related laws and regulations. Today, however, they are still being concluded, even though various pollution-related laws and regulations have been issued. Around two thousand agreements are concluded every year.

There are two reasons for this:

- First, anti-pollution agreements make it possible to implement detailed pollution prevention and control measures well suited to the geographical and social conditions in each city; and
- Second, business enterprises have become aware that obtaining the consent of the community residents where they locate their plants is necessary for achieving smooth and harmonious business activity.

Anti-pollution agreements are also useful in new areas of environmental problems where adequate measures have not yet been prepared by laws and regulations.

for built up areas. Consciousness in planning may thus have an influence on energy consumption and energy costs.

The factors influencing running costs which should be taken into account in decisions on the siting of residential areas include microclimate, location in relation to public transport and existing municipal networks, and the possibility of utilising existing services. These factors correspond to 40 per cent of the running costs for residential areas. Especially in general planning, where the siting of important functions is outlined, it is important to note the structure of running costs and the possibilities for reducing them.

In the Finnish residential areas studied, the running costs are on average 3.8 per cent of the building costs, which means that in some 25 years the running costs will rise to the same as the building costs. Without leading to adverse environmental effects, economy in planning may lead to annual savings of over one million MK in the total costs for residential areas. Substantial savings, therefore, can be made if land use planning and energy planning are systematically combined.

In Norway, relevant planning measures include using the authority provided by the Planning and Building Act to prepare national provisions for the co-ordination of land use, roads and transport planning. The aim is to encourage more effective and environmentally-positive traffic development.

Environmental impact assessment

The availability of information on the environmental impact of various proposed activities in urban areas would help to stimulate debate and, in the longer term, lead to more rational and consistent decision-making. In some countries (e.g. as in the case of the federal requirements in the United States for environmental impact statements for publicly sponsored projects) this is done systematically. Information is, however, not always so freely available on some of the key components of the urban system, especially as environmental impact assessment is rarely undertaken at this level.

In many countries, for example, there is no single record of urban land ownership (which is essentially for cadastral purposes as much as for wider policy debate) and, indeed, there may (as in the United Kingdom) be no publicly available information source at all for some land. Information of this type is, however, available in various forms in some OECD countries. Denmark, for instance, has published land valuation data for over 50 years, Austria publishes such information, while Japan ensures that all land sales are registered and published. Full cadastral surveys exist in Sweden. Information on land ownership is important if many of the tools of environmental policy are to be fully effective and trends in environmental indicators are to be monitored.

Consideration, therefore, needs to be given to the explicit incorporation of environmental assessment procedures into the everyday operations of city development and planning. Such procedures would allow for the consistent consideration by both the community and its administrators of the environmental considerations of urban development proposals. At present environmental impact assessment, although adopted by most OECD countries, is not used widely at the urban level.

Information programmes

Better information is increasingly regarded as an important instrument of environmental policy. Action can be immensely varied. It may simply involve advice to property owners about the maintenance of property, to commercial operators about the better management of their waste disposal handling, to car drivers about parking arrangements. Advice of this kind is a prerequisite for environmental good behaviour. But to change behaviour it may be necessary to go further and run campaigns to raise awareness. For example, in the United Kingdom, Environment Week has been organised by the National Civic Trust Organisation since 1984 as one week in the spring when local authorities, businesses, schools, community organisations and the media are invited and encouraged to initiate environmental improvements.

Moral suasion, coupled with carefully couched arguments about private interests, can prove a useful tool in bringing private sector investment into the process of urban regeneration in cases where a city is severely run-down. Arguments concerning social responsibility can be deployed, but more important is the need to convince private concerns that they would actually benefit from an improved urban environment, especially from a reduction in the legacy effects. Award schemes and competitions can similarly be used to raise awareness, and also aspirations and standards. There has been a large expansion of environmental awards in the United Kingdom in the last decade, most of them organised by professional, trade or voluntary organisations with business sponsorship. More fundamentally, attitudes and values can be changed by education. Environmental education, both within and outside the school curriculum, has developed strongly in the last decade offering training for teachers and courses for students and preparing teaching material.

In effect, there are few commercial benefits from piecemeal action – it is unlikely to reduce the individual concern's costs of production or improve its market – but concerted actions by a large consortium of private companies effectively internalise within the group the benefits of a rejuvenated economy. In a sense, the policy tool is one akin to that of "indicative planning". By information programmes, persuasion and, possibly, a number of public sector schemes the authority convinces the private sector of the merits of combined action to remove contaminated soil, restore building, invest in new infrastructure and create more jobs.

Evaluating instrument effectiveness

The aim of urban environmental policy should be to maximise the net benefits of the urban population by influencing the quality of the environment and urban economic development. Similarly, any given policy package must be the least-cost package for a given level of welfare creation. What this means is that the costs of adopting the various instruments discussed previously need to be aggregated for various mixes of instruments, whilst the ways in which the aggregate costs vary for different levels of policy achievement also need to be investigated.

Rather than trying to target individual policy instruments, it might be more fruitful to consider the "portfolio" of instruments which is likely to prove most efficient at handling the adverse environmental effects encountered in an urban area at a particular time.

The acceptability of a system depends not only upon its complexity (or simplicity) but also on the extent to which the parties have consulted each other on the design and application of the instruments. In France and the Netherlands, for example, water pollution charge schemes are reasonably well accepted because there is extensive consultation between central government, industry, local authorities and users.

The application of economic instruments can be greatly facilitated if existing financial and tax channels can be used. In the future, however, it may be necessary to redefine the taxation mechanism if environmental costs are to be truly internalised. In addition, the redistributive character of certain instruments (redistribution of sums collected as charges) can make them much more acceptable, especially where the methods and purposes of redistribution have been explained and negotiated among the interested parties.

User charges are of particular importance when improvements to the environment of a given urban area yield welfare benefits to non-residents. This is the "suburban-central city exploitation" issue, whereby city taxpayers effectively provide services for outside individuals who thus "free-ride" on the services. The relevance of this issue lies in its implications for local government finance. Strict adoption of the "user-pays-principle" could reduce central city taxes in favour of outsiders paying the full cost of the services from which they benefit.

In addition, a number of innovative mechanisms for taxation also exist for protecting the urban environment. At present, most taxation measures are targeted at resource ownership (e.g. building tax and car ownership tax) rather than at resource use. Taxation measures targeted at resource use would more directly recognise and account for the potential environmental damages which may be caused by such use. In particular, land use taxation on derelict land and vehicle use taxation should be given greater consideration.

In conclusion, the greater use of economic instruments will make a major contribution to the "external" integration of environmental policies with other policies such as those for energy, transport and land use at the urban level. An economic approach is particularly suitable for integrating urban environmental policies because it offers scope for adjusting taxes and charges so as to benefit the urban environment. It is recognised that regulations will always be important and a harmony between the two mechanisms that best achieves the desired objectives is required. A recent OECD publication on the application of "Economic Instruments for Environmental Protection" (1989) recommends that administrators considering the implementation and enforcement of economic instruments should remember the following points:

- The objectives of economic instruments should be clear;
- Instruments should be simple in introduction and operation;
- Instruments should be acceptable to target groups;
- Economic instruments in mixed systems should fit in with regulations and with the existing administrative, political and judicial framework;
- Charges should be compatible with existing tax systems, if possible;
- Instruments should facilitate regulatory reform and should introduce more flexibility in regulations;
- There should be compatibility with supranational agreements and principles, such as the "polluter-pays principle".

Chapter 4

NEW INITIATIVES FOR OLD PROBLEMS – URBAN AREA REHABILITATION, URBAN TRANSPORT AND URBAN ENERGY

Although a large number of urban environmental issues are currently of concern to OECD countries, it would be too lengthy a task to discuss them all in this report. Only those environmental policies and programmes which have an urban scope and approach are described here. Sectoral policies on air pollution abatement, noise control, waste and water management, etc. have been assessed separately in several recent OECD reports and are still ongoing areas of work in OECD.

So as to give an indication of the types of initiatives and actions being undertaken in specific areas, this chapter focuses on three urban environmental issues – rehabilitation, transport and energy. The emphasis is on identifying innovative approaches and the lessons to be learnt with respect to financing, short and long term impacts and political feasibility.

1. URBAN AREA REHABILITATION

The issue

National economies and cities in OECD countries are currently undergoing a number of structural changes to which cities must adapt if they are to remain efficient locations for economic activity. This adaptation is not just a matter of economic efficiency in a narrow sense, as there is clearly a recognisable demand from citizens to live in, and for business to locate in, high quality environments – physical, social and cultural.

Problems of urban area rehabilitation affect not only declining cities but also growing cities. A prosperous city can generate problems of urban sprawl and thereby create pressure on agricultural land. In addition, rapidly growing cities can outpace investment in necessary infrastructure and thereby create excessive strain on existing urban services such as water, waste and transport services. Urban change creates a wide range of different problems for different types of cities. It is the problems of adapting cities to structural change, particularly adapting from older, traditional manufacturing activities to service activities that is a key concern in many OECD countries. In southern European countries, for example Spain, structural change has led to the degradation of historical centres and contributed to poverty in these areas. The factors that may combine to bring about urban degradation from this process are outlined in Figure 3.

Figure 3. **URBAN DEGRADATION: THE INCREASING PROBLEM**

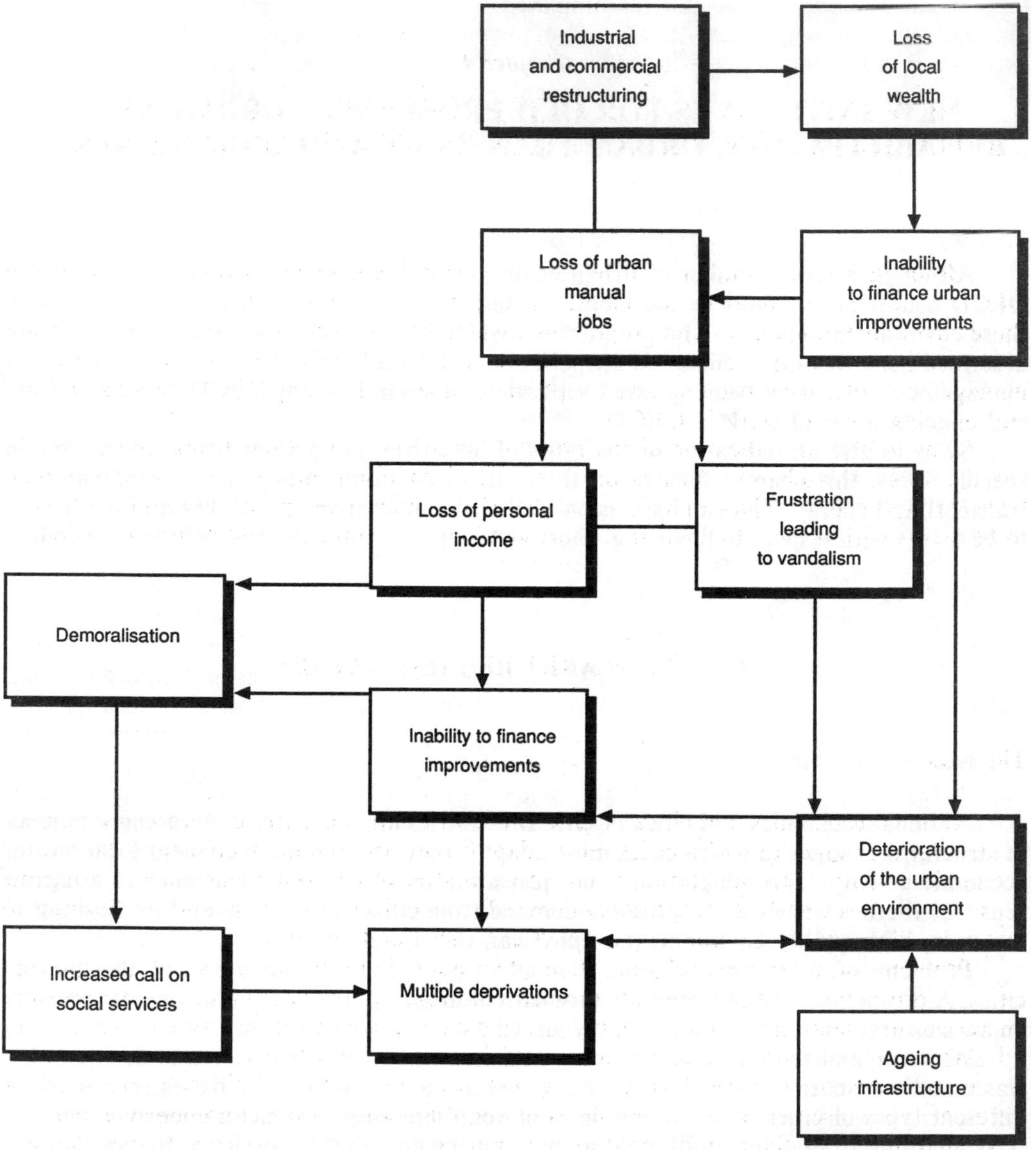

In certain areas, for example in False Creek in Vancouver, Canada or Salford Quays in Greater Manchester, United Kingdom, the decline in traditional activities had become almost complete, leaving very large areas (200 ha in False Creek) unused or underused. The more traditional heavy industries leave behind a legacy of sites which are extremely costly to develop because of, for instance, the need to remove deep foundations, remnant large engineering structures and contaminated land. However, the problems of restructuring and replacing older more traditional manufacturing and related activities with newer activities is to be found in growing cities as much as in older declining industrial centres, as for example, the Golden Horn Development Project in Istanbul, Turkey, illustrates. In Barcelona, Spain, urban degradation of the historical inner centre has led to large scale renovation projects to restore new life to its past glory and also house some of the poor population.

In addition to the size of the areas affected, the timescale of decline and renewal in such areas is also significant – taking tens of years. The process of decline itself is slow; moreover, the scale of these areas is such that it can take 10-30 years to fully redevelop them.

Clearly the impact of change is much wider than a physical legacy of decay and dereliction. The decline in activities also results in major job losses and hence high levels of unemployment in neighbouring areas, with all the associated social problems. (For a more detailed discussion of this aspect, see 'Managing Urban Change', Vol.1, OECD, 1983.)

The majority of urban renewal/rehabilitation cases are examples of redevelopment in major waterside locations, whether located in old industrial areas or in cities facing other aspects of structural change. They demonstrate the current structural trend of the replacement of coastal heavy industries (ports, riverside industry and their associated infrastructure) which have become redundant or inefficient, with newer, primarily service activities (leisure, offices, recreation and housing). The change is from a functional use of water to an aesthetic and recreational use. In many instances this has required expenditure not only for site reclamation but also to improve water quality and reduce pollution levels. This is an important aspect of projects in Rotterdam, Netherlands, Salford Quays, Unitd Kingdom, and Vancouver, Canada. Other important renewal/rehabilitation initiatives have been associated with the preservation of historical centres and town character, for example in Mons, Belgium, in Barcelona, Spain, and in Perugia, Italy.

Processes of decline, renewal and change of use are constantly under way in cities. What makes these areas stand out is their size and the difficult problems of rehabilitating sites with major derelict engineering structures or buildings and, often, contaminated sites. The decline of a whole quarter of a city means that new piecemeal investment is deterred because the dereliction of adjacent sites undermines the value of any new individual investment. Hence the externalities of dereliction set up a spiral of reduced investment or disinvestment and loss of confidence. In inner city areas, considerable effort has gone into reversing this spiral and creating the confidence that new investment will be supported by improvements in the area rather than undermined by further decline.

Whilst it is clear that the largescale decline of certain city areas is due to the operation of economic structural change, with loss of demand for traditional activities reinforced by the externalities of lack of investment in premises, there must also be an underlying market demand for the new service activities. The question is, how are these demands to be harnessed and focused on derelict urban quarters?

A number of measures need to be considered (Figure 4). To renew or rehabilitate an area in decline it may be necessary to provide appropriate local urban management frameworks, resources and incentives to support new small and medium-sized businesses

Figure 4. **URBAN DEGRADATION: IMPROVING THE ENVIRONMENT**

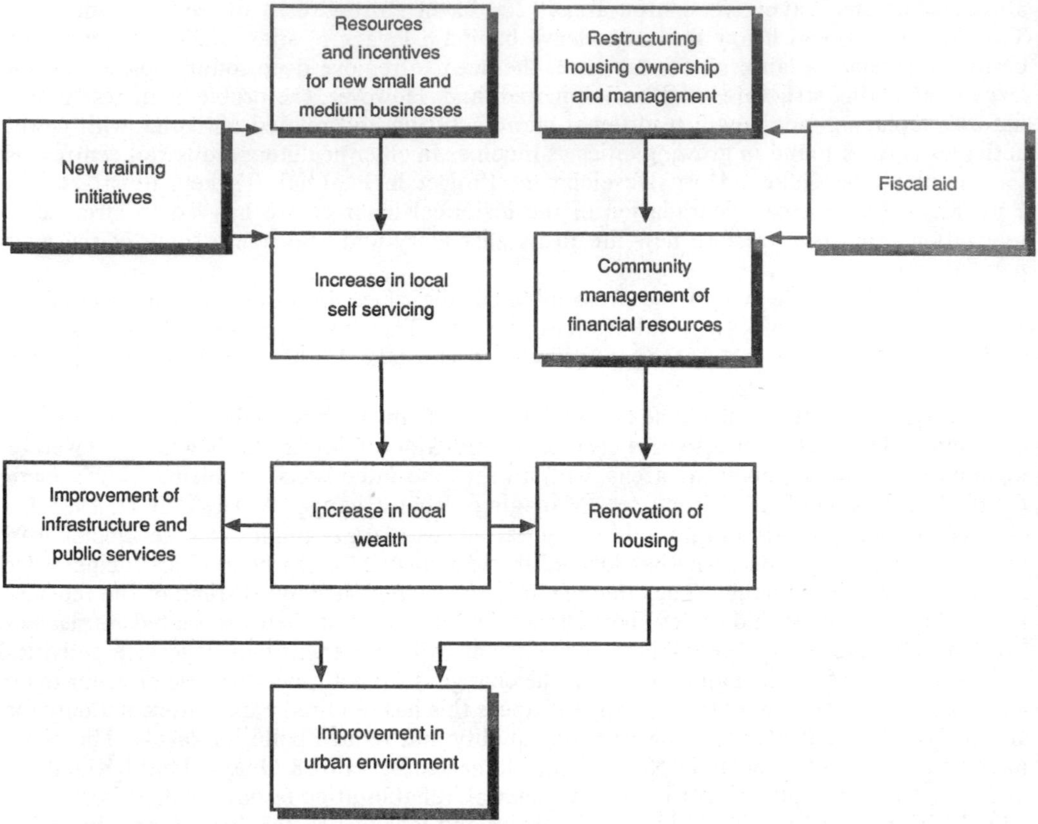

and housing ownership. In addition, greater autonomy could be given to cities to manage fiscal resources so that they could self-service their own needs. Such an approach might help to reverse environmental degradation in city areas.

Innovative approaches

Present urban renewal and rehabilitation initiatives undertaken in OECD countries all demonstrate how environmental quality, or the confidence that it will be provided, plays a significant role in encouraging redevelopment. They also demonstrate the corollary that new, major developments and renovation can help to rehabilitate the environment. In every case they demonstrate success in: finding new uses for derelict/declining areas; helping to regenerate land values; improving the environment; providing new jobs and employment; increasing income in the area; and having a wider impact on the surrounding area. Collectively they show that investment in environmental improvement is no longer a burden for economic development and that for some of the newer technological service-based industries, a healthy urban environment is a prerequisite for investment.

Success achieved in initial projects also increased the confidence of local leaders and communities and enabled them to respond successfully to other challenges. For example, in Vancouver, Canada (Inset 5), and Salford Quays, United Kingdom (Inset 6), the initial renewal projects were not only inportant for their own sake but also helped to catalyse similarly dramatic environmental upgrading on other nearby sites.

A number of common ingredients for successful urban rehabilitation programmes can be identified. These are:

- The preparation of a supportive local plan;
- Adequate resources and time horizon;
- Public authority initiative and pump priming;
- Public/private/community partnerships in implementation;
- Local implementation; and
- Large land holdings.

Renewal or rehabilitation plan

The key aspects of the successful plans were that they all:

- Assessed the area's strengths and weaknesses;
- Helped to identify a new role in the area;
- Set multiple objectives for the area; and
- Included a range of elements (land uses, environmental quality criteria and design, employment and training initiatives, social and cultural facilities).

For example, one of the keys to success in Winnipeg's core area initiative, Canada, was the application of what is a rather orthodox tenet of urban planning theory but one that is rarely practised: that urban problems are all interrelated and must be approached on a holistic rather than a fragmented and uni-dimensional basis. Thus environmental, physical, economic, and social problems were all attacked simultaneously, in as comprehensive and integrated manner as humanly possible. One of the keys for success is the forging of a single, highly visible, and relatively cohesive project identity for an extremely diverse set of activities. This was partly responsible for the success of the Rotterdam project, Netherlands. In addition, the successful restoration of Mons, Belgium, is a reflection of the implementation of a flexible structure plan which combined housing, green space, preservation and traffic policies. Importantly, the Mons strategy is one of active "integrated conservation" at the urban level. The basis of the plan is to have greater respect for existing urban structures; to let historical legacy influence choice of function; to ensure architectural continuity; and to use quality of city life as a basic development and planning yardstick.

The plans provide a framework for generating confidence. Potential private sector developers and investors, local firms and residents can see the final vision for the area. Given that commitment for implementing a plan is demonstrated, then potential partners have greater confidence that their efforts and investments would be enhanced and protected by complementary activity and investment taking place elsewhere in the area.

Financial resources and time horizon

A corollary of the scale of the problem faced in these areas is that the resources required and the time scale taken for renewal are equally large. These need to be reflected

Inset 5. **Environmental Initiatives with Urban Development – The Case of False Creek, Vancouver, Canada**

A century ago, the False Creek Basin was a clean, sparkling inlet of the Pacific Ocean filled with fish and surrounded by gigantic fir trees. Shortly thereafter, a rapid environmental decline of the area began as extensive logging took place, the Canadian Pacific Railway located its marhsalling yards on the north side of False Creek and heavy industry became operative.

With popular support, multiple partnerships of government and the private sector have transformed False Creek from a rundown industrial wasteland into a vibrant mixed use area which includes a residential neighbourhood, community amenities, commercial enterprise, cultural activity, parkland, waterfront and open space. False Creek was the site of Expo 86, the world trade exposition.

The south shore of False Creek, the first stage of the Basin's redevelopment, was initiated and led by a local government, the City of Vancouver. It proceeded in three phases, from 1968 until 1982 when the last phase was completed. Social objectives such as community structure constituted the focus of the project. Many environmental improvements accompanied the transformation of thirty-two hectares of derelict industrial land into public use and 1 800 units of housing containing a mix of incomes, family types, ages, and tenancy forms.

Granville Island, the second redevelopment project in the False Creek area, was initiated in 1982. It is a 17-hectare waterfront site adjacent to the south shore of False Creek. The federal government assumed the lead role in the redevelopment of the island using a Crown corporation (a company in the ordinary sense of the term, but whose sole shareholder is the government), Canada Mortgage and Housing Corporation. The site was transformed into a "people place" providing social, cultural, educational, retail and other activities. Residential land use was not an objective of development and the Island has become a major attraction for both tourists and Vancouverites.

The North Shore project, the third and largest initiative, is still under way and is expected to take about 15 more years. Over 80 hectares of land will have been redeveloped when the project is completed. Initially, the provincial government took the lead role through a Crown corporation. The objectives of the project included the preparation of the site for EXPO 86, the construction of a sports stadium, new housing, and retail and office space.

A review of the three management processes underlying the large-scale redevelopment projects has identified the following conclusions which may be transferable to other cities:

1. Large-scale redevelopment projects containing social objectives must be initiated by the government.
2. Private sector participation stretches public funds, improves cost-effectiveness and increases the scale on which environmental upgrading is affordable. Private developers contributed directly to the many environmental improvements through the development process itself, and indirectly by the leveraging of their investments – that is, private sector investment stimulated by government "seed money". The relatively high leverage ratios of private sector investment and the presence of revenue-generating activities (primarily leasing of land) enabled the government to assemble land, replace obsolescent infrastructure, provide services, and to undertake major environmental improvements at very little cost.
3. Consolidated land ownership (private or public) is a prerequisite to planning and development. On the South Shore, the decision to lease parcels of land to the private developer gave the government agency greater control, and ensured that public policy objectives would be realised and sustained.
4. Delegation of authority to a locally-based management team improves the efficiency and flexibility of the process. The agencies responsible for South False Creek and Granville Island were able to develop flexible planning and implementation procedures that adapted to the individual needs of a particular tenant, as long as the original goals of the project were satisfied.
5. Harmonious intergovernmental relations in redevelopment projects with social objectives are crucial. An examination of South False Creek reveals that the financial contributions of various federal and provincial programmes were essential to the achievement of the population and age-mix objectives.
6. Major redevelopment projects require a long time for implementation and for the realisation of all benefits. A long time frame also requires a patient investor, as returns from the original investment may not be fully realised until the project is well established. The spin-off benefits in the adjacent communities of False Creek are only now beginning to be evident.

Inset 6. **Large Scale Renewal of Derelict Docklands – The Case of Salford Quays, Greater Manchester, United Kingdom**

Salford Docks and the Manchester Ship Canal were opened in 1894 by Queen Victoria and played a vital role in the growth of the region for nearly a century. In recent times they have gone into decline and the heart of what was once the nation's third largest port now lies derelict and vacant. Extending over more than 150 acres of land, 75 acres of water and 3 miles of open water front, they represent a unique development opportunity at the heart of the conurbation.

These opportunities are demonstrated by the development which has taken place over the last three years. The compelling need to realise the hidden economic and environmental opportunities which existed at the heart of the docks prompted Salford City Council to prepare a redevelopment plan for the Salford Docks.

The designation of part of the Docks as an Enterprise Zone helped to initiate private development interest. This was encouraged by the City Council through a land deal with a developer and grant assistance towards reclamation works and service provision by central government. This initial co-operation between different levels of government and a key entrepreneur helped to stimulate major private sector investment.

The City of Salford has co-ordinated and managed the overall programme of infrastructure provision and private development. Strong commitment and leadership by the Mayor and the Chief Executive of the Council have ensured the success of the project. A Corporate Management Sub-committee was established to take and enact all key decisions on the redevelopment project. This enabled a co-ordinated approach to decisions to be maintained at a political level, exercising an important influence on the Salford Quays Project and the way it was developed. A streamlined political process, allied with a co-ordinated technical programme, proved to be essential to achieving results. The reclamation of the former docks to become Salford Quays has proceeded to programme: new roads, canals and walkways have been constructed; services such as water, electricity, gas and sewers installed; trees planted and landscaping undertaken; former cranes and a redundant railway bridge have been moved and renovated. The water areas have been separated from the Ship Canal and, using aeration techniques, are being improved for leisure and recreation use.

Private investment is also occurring. During a period of high unemployment, a large number of new industries have been introduced or moved into the area. These include food processing and precision engineering, printing, telecommunications, and service industries such as retail distribution, building contractors, commercial photography, dental laboratories, design consultants and office interiors. These are mainly new to Salford and will be important in future years in diversifying the industrial and commercial base of the City's employment structure.

Salford Quays has provided a new image for the City of Salford by encouraging new investment based on environmental improvement. This redevelopment has, in turn, encouraged new development in adjacent areas. Local government in partnership with central government and the private sector can achieve economic and environmental regeneration if there is a will to succeed and funding is available, and if there is a commitment to undertake and complete the task. Success in these terms has proven immensely beneficial to the local authority, its business community and its residents.

not simply in the plan but in the commitment of resources and in implementation. It is important to realise that the long time frame frequently associated with the completion of large scale urban projects may also apply to the pay back period, or the time it takes for investors to realise a profit. Returns from the original investment may not be fully realised until the project is well established. In addition, although government money is important, it should be realised that its availability is an insufficient prerequisite to successful large scale redevelopment initiatives. It is the way it is invested, in addition to how much is invested, that is crucial. Private investment can be levered into action with relatively small amounts of government seed money, provided the lever is strategically placed in respect of locations and uses attractive to profit-motivated ventures.

Such commitment once sustained is likely to generate large scale economic investment in the area that more than pays back the initial public investment. For example, in Vancouver, Canada, the city's initial investment of $20M in land and infrastructure helped to stimulate roughly $135M in additional investment by private and non-profit developers on the South Shore alone. This leverage factor of nearly 7:1 begins to suggest the enormous positive economic impact which well-conceived and executed urban redevelopment projects can have in addition to the dramatic improvements which they produce in urban environmental quality.

Very often, this commitment to long term implementation is manifest in the setting up of a special executive body charged with implementation of the plan over a 5-, 10-, or 20-year period and invested with resources and relevant powers (e.g. land assembly, development, plan-making powers). For example in the Winnipeg Core Area Initiative, Canada, a further key to success was the creation of a special-purpose central agency with the time, resources and mandate to preoccupy itself exclusively with the core area: the "Core Area Office", whose sole raison d'etre was the mobilisation, focusing, and delivery of public and private investment in the core area. In the absence of such an agency, it is quite probable that the more traditional centrifugal tendencies of both the marketplace and the line departments of the three levels of government would have prevailed, and dramatically reduced the project's impact.

Public authority initiative and pump priming

Given the size of the areas requiring renewal/rehabilitation and their need for infrastructure reclamation and environmental works, in addition to the normal investments, all of the urban rehabilitation areas present a difficult challenge. Therefore public authorities have had to take the initiative in proposing action for renewal/rehabilitation, setting in train planning and partnership arrangements and, of prime importance, demonstrating commitment by allocating and spending public funds to start the process of change. Such expenditure has been used for a wide range of purposes including: site reclamation; tax breaks for investors; environmental improvements; public/low cost housing provision; provision of public parks, walkways, cultural and community facilities; and infrastructure.

Partnership in implementation

Without exception, all of the projects noted here emphasize the importance of partnership in implementing the plan. These partnerships are often represented in the constitution of the executive bodies referred to above. Partnerships vary widely in range and form. They include partnerships between city or metropolitan authorities and other levels of government and partnerships between government departments. In every case, a vitally important element in the partnership has been the private sector in the form of land owners, developers, investors, and industrialists in the area. Finally, in a number of cases local residents, voluntary and non-profit groups have also played a significant partnership role in the formulation and implementation of plans.

Local implementation

Each case study demonstrated that the most effective way of responding to the challenge in these areas is to implement renewal/rehabilitation strategies at the local level and often through a specially constituted body. Local implementation enables those responsible to be close to the area so that they can recognise and respond to opportunities that arise; can tailor action to local conditions; and can more easily form partnerships with local firms, private sector interests and residents. Furthermore, if power for implementation is situated locally, then decisions can be made quickly and the body can be more responsive to local demands and propositions that arise.

For example, in the Toronto Harbourfront project, Canada, over the first three years, an enormous amount of planning and consultative activity was undertaken under the aegis of the federal government, but very little in the way of substance occurred. One of the principal reasons for this was the virtual exclusion of the City of Toronto from the consultative process. The federal government's response to this was to set up an informal "Harbourfront Council" whose nominees included officials of all three levels of government and to appoint a senior City of Toronto official as general manager of the project. These actions have stimulated the desired implementation results.

Large land holdings

In every case, the process of urban change was made easier to implement because much of the derelict land was held by a few large land owners, both public and private. Very often land swaps, deals or pooling, rationalised these holdings and further assisted development. This was an important aspect of the success of the renewal projects in Canada. Similarly, in the Vienna-Danube project, Austria, the restructuring of the riverine area for flood control and recreational and leisure activities would not have been successful without the combination of local and national authority land holding interests.

Future challenges

The processes of structural and locational change will continue and hence the demand for major public sector commitment is likely to continue. In many instances, urban revitalisation strategies result in a complete change of economic activity in the areas renewed – from manufacturing to services – and also, in some cases, a rapid rise in property and house prices. However, it is not clear in every case that former residents of the area or those living nearby and who used to be employed in these areas are now benefiting from the change. The challenge is to ensure that the benefits of new employment opportunities, better income, environment and housing are also made available to those who formerly depended upon the area. To ensure this, schemes should include special training programmes and provision for social housing.

In addition, in many instances the effects of concerted action and public sector pump priming are to revitalise areas and eventually raise land values. In some instances, the public sector benefits from this where it holds land for development. However, the public sector is often also the major holder of land for parks and environmental improvement; its value cannot be realised but helps to increase the value of adjacent private sector plots. In instances where much of the increase in values benefits private sector owners, means should be found to "claw back" some of this increased value for the public sector to repay its initial pump priming expenditure.

Finally, as urban revitalisation is a continuing process the question arises, is it possible to find means of ensuring that cities will not, in the future, be left with large areas that have to be reclaimed using public sector funds. Attention should be addressed to the means of internalising these costs within the market. A number of economic instruments suggest themselves: the posting of bonds against clean-up when development permission is granted; the charging of a contingency tax or a tax on betterment value when planning permission is given.

2. URBAN TRANSPORT

The issue

Efficient transport is an integral part of economic development. Although there are various theories on the detailed role transport plays in the development process, it is agreed that it provides the means for factors of production to be brought together in the production process and for the final products to be distributed to consumers. Transport is particularly important in the context of urban economic growth, both in terms of ensuring the efficiency of the internal workings of the urban economy and as the means by which urban areas can interact with the wider national and international economy. Transport is, therefore, one of the major activities within an urban area. The actual amount of urban traffic has increased considerably in recent years (25 per cent within the last 10 years) as car ownership has risen and road transport has increased in importance as a means of freight movement.

Trends in energy consumption in transport are very different from the other energy sectors. In the United Kingdom, for example, between 1973 and 1984 energy use in transport increased by over 16 per cent whilst non-transport consumption fell by 19 per cent. In the United States, transport uses account for nearly one-quarter of all the energy used in the the country, with automobile responsible for over 75 per cent of that consumption. Although considerable improvements in energy efficiency have been made by vehicle manufacturers, through better design and the use of new materials, there has been relatively little emphasis to date on improving efficiency through better transport use.

The environmental impacts of transport are extensive and land transport is one of the major contributors to atmospheric pollution. In Greece, for example, transport contributes 86.4 per cent of the tonnage of air pollutants in the Athens basin. Transport also makes extensive use of scarce, non renewable resources, especially carbon fuels. Transport in this sense, therefore, contributes to environmental degradation on a global scale, in the sense that it directly affects the overall well-being of society as a whole.

For those living in cities, the environmental impact of transport takes on additional dimensions. Apart from atmospheric pollution and resource depletion, there are local problems of vibration, noise, safety, community severance, visual intrusion and congestion. Concern about these latter effects can influence decisions about residential and industrial location. In turn, these locational factors can affect the economic vitality of an urban area. The range of factors that have contributed to the increasing problems associated with transport use are set out in Figure 5. Rising car ownership and use, and a reduction (or inadequate increase) in public transport provision have formed a vicious circle, leading to increased fuel consumption, increased air pollution, increased pressure on land (through dispersal of land uses) and increased problems of access for those without vehicles.

Transport, therefore, poses several specific sub-problems. Firstly, within the urban area itself one of the major causes of environmental damage is mobile and thus spatially specific

Figure 5. **TRANSPORT POLLUTION: THE INCREASING PROBLEM**

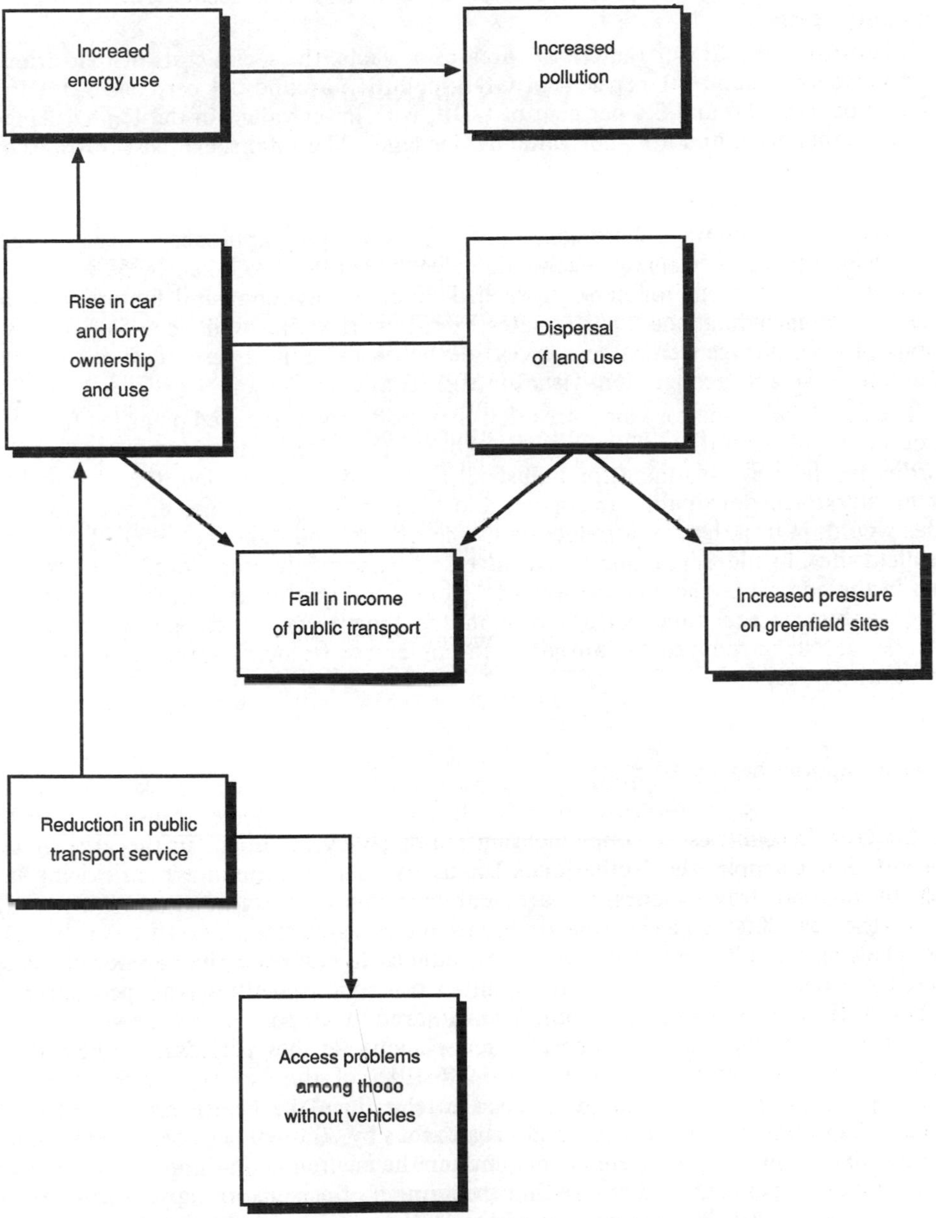

policies may simply result in a displacement within the city of the source of the problem. Secondly, policies applied in any one urban area to curtail the use of transport on environmental grounds may simply lead to a shift of the source of the problem to other urban areas or to areas outside the cities. Finally, transport requires large amounts of unsightly infrastructure, generating its own problems involving aesthetics (the scenic vista) and physical community severance.

It is estimated that, for the OECD area as a whole, the social costs of road transport due to noise are around 0.1 per cent of GDP; pollution around 0.4 per cent of GDP; and accidents between 2.0 and 2.4 per cent of GDP, with lower values in the United Kingdom and the Netherlands, and a higher value in Germany. The total social cost of transport in these three countries is estimated at between 2.5 and 3.0 per cent of GDP (figures calculated by the OECD Environment Directorate).

Looked at in this way, those concerned with developing appropriate urban transport policies which permit sustainable economic development need to take a wide view of what constitutes the urban environment. A diverse range of environmental factors need to be accounted for, including: noise; particulates; vibration; risk; fuel additive emissions; concentrations of CO; nitrogen emissions; excess depletion of natural resources; urban sprawl; community severance; congestion; visual intrusion; and aesthetics.

The fiscal and regulatory measures that may bring about reduced pollution from traffic and other environmental benefits are outlined in Figure 6. Restrictions on car and truck use, co-ordinated land use planning for industrial and residential location, the channelling of greater investment into public transport, and a more integrative use of public transport modes would, in turn, lead to a reduction in energy use, pollution and reduced pressure on greenfield sites. In addition, reducing the adverse environmental impacts of urban transport, taken in the context of the links between environmental quality and location, may in itself lead to enhanced economic performance in the long term. In recognition of this, the Netherlands has introduced the authority to implement traffic measures solely with environmental purposes.

Innovative approaches

All OECD countries are implementing major policy initiatives in the area of urban transport. For example, the Netherlands has as its goal: to introduce road pricing in the 1990s to influence travel modes, in particular on home-work traffic regulations; to eliminate, by the year 2000, unacceptable air pollution levels generated by traffic in urban areas; noise levels as a result from traffic are to be reduced to eliminate the number of seriously affected persons by the year 2010; the number of traffic casualties is to be reduced, the number of dead by 50 per cent, the number of injured by 40 per cent by the year 2010; and the provision of public space for car parking, especially for long periods, is to be restricted. Similarly, the long-term programme for 1986-1989 of the Norwegian State Pollution Authority states, inter alia, that its goals are to: reduce the health impacts of exhaust emissions from private cars in towns and urban areas by 70 to 90 per cent in relation to the prognoses based on present developments; reduce the environmental impacts of Norwegian road traffic by 50 per cent; and ensure that the number of persons strongly troubled by noise and smell from road traffic does not exceed the 1985 level. In addition, Sweden has a goal of reducing NO_x emissions from traffic by at least 30 per cent and SO_2 emissions by 65 per cent by 1995.

Figure 6. **TRANSPORT POLLUTION: IMPROVING THE ENVIRONMENT**

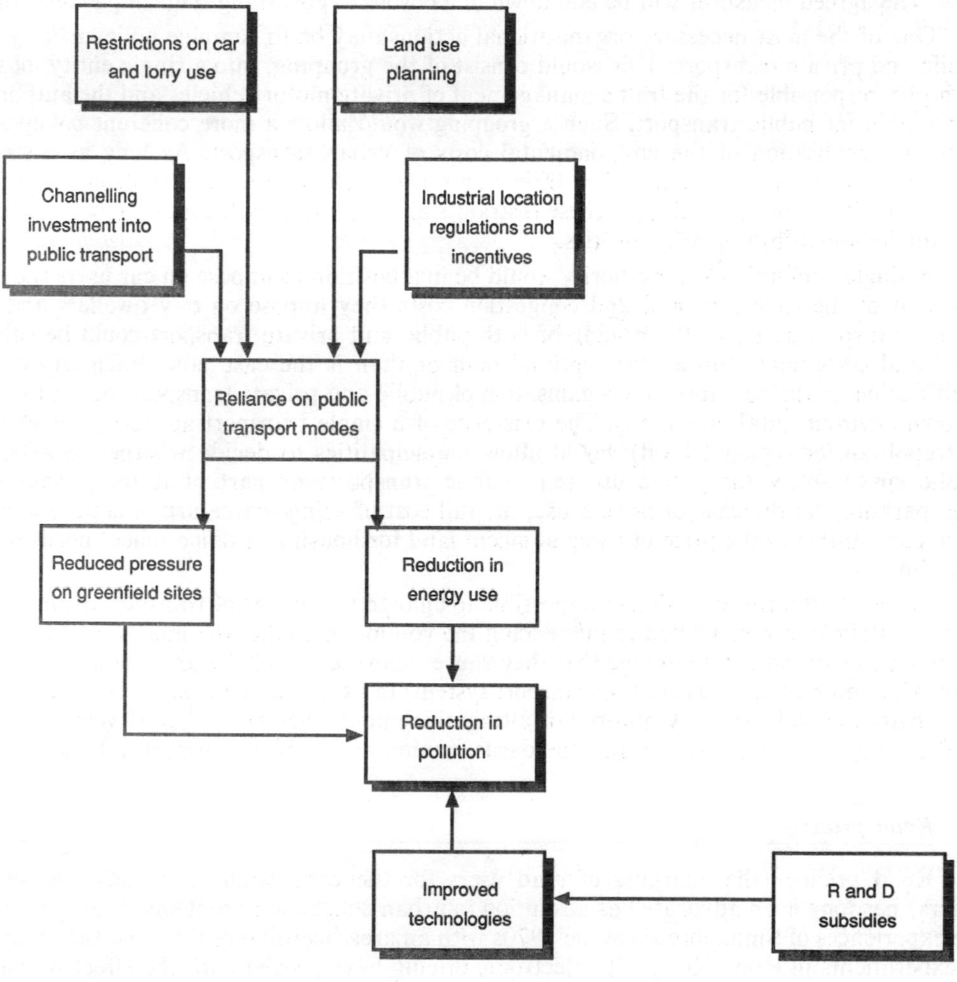

In the most successful cases of environmentally positive transport policies, integration and its organisational aspects (as outlined in Chapter 3) have played a primary role. For example, in the Netherlands, research commissioned by the Ministry of Transport and Public Works on the possibilities of solving the growing length and incidence of traffic queues on the Randstad motorway system led to the conclusion that local or single sector measures were inadequate. The implementation of an integrated package of measures required the co-operation of municipal, provincial and national authorities as well as semi-private and private institutions. The composition of the "accessibility plan" for the

Randstad was agreed upon between these parties. The implementation of the scheme is also to take place in close co-operation. Mixed project teams of officials have been installed, their proposals are submitted to an executive consultation group consisting of the Minister of Transport and Public Works, and representatives of the provincial and municipal executives. The agreed measures will be laid down in a covenant governing their implementation.

One of the most necessary organisational actions may be to combine policymaking for public and private transport. This would consist of the grouping, into a single entity, of the authority responsible for the traffic management of private motor vehicles and the authority responsible for public transport. Such a grouping would allow a more coherent policy and better internalisation of the environmental costs of urban transport. As long as a single authority does not exist, the use of restraints on private vehicles and of incentives for public transport will not be optimal since these restraints and incentives will continue to be decided and implemented by separate entities.

A single comprehensive authority would be in a position to impose on car users the full payment of the environmental and congestion costs they impose on city dwellers and on public transport users, as the pricing of both public and private transport could be calculated and co-ordinated in a more optimal manner than is the case now. Each city could itself decide on the best mix and organisation of public and private transport, depending on its own environmental conditions. The existence of a single transport authority (at urban, metropolitan, or regional level) would allow municipalities to decide whether to allocate public space solely for public use (e.g. public transport) or part of it for private use (e.g. parking). In the case of private use, the full cost of using scarce urban land (e.g. at a price comparable to the price of using adjacent land for housing or office space) needs to be charged.

In the short term, it is almost impossible to change the modes of transport available in an area. Policies are restricted to influencing the volume of traffic, the modes used and the immediate environmental damage that they cause. Short term policies are essentially aimed at making more efficient use of the transport systems in situ, more efficient in both economic and environmental terms. A number of alternative approaches have been developed using road pricing, emissions pricing and standards, zoning and public transport enhancement.

Road pricing

Road pricing (the charging of road users for the congestion costs they impose on others) has long been advocated as a solution to urban congestion problems. More recently, the experiences of Singapore since the 1970s with an area licensing regime and the outcome of experiments in Hong Kong with electronic pricing have proved both the effectiveness of such a policy and the technical possibilities of more advanced systems. Road pricing has been traditionally seen as a means of improving the engineering efficiency of the transport network (which will of itself save fuel). However, evidence in Stockholm, Sweden, suggests that road pricing systems also have considerable merit as an instrument for internalising the social costs associated with the deterioration of the physical environment. In the Stockholm study, it is estimated that a cordon road pricing scheme involving a 25 SK fee per car per round trip would reduce nitrogen oxide emissions by 12 per cent and carbon monoxide emissions by 73 per cent in Stockholm County (Inset 7). There is also evidence from Bergen, Norway, where a similar type of scheme is in operation, albeit as part of a revenue raising programme for infrastructure building, that not only does road pricing reduce traffic volumes in the urban area (by about 6-7 per cent) but that the concept has gained a high

Inset 7. **Evaluation of the Combination of an Area Licensing Scheme and Different Public Transport Subsidies as Environmental Policy Measures in Stockholm County, Sweden**

In recent years, environmental and ecological quality have become important social and political issues in Sweden. The contribution of car traffic to air pollution and its associated negative environmental impacts has long been recognised. On the advice from Sweden's National Environmental Agency, the Swedish parliament set a national goal to reduce emissions of different pollutants, including nitrogen oxides (NO_x), by 30 per cent from the level in 1980 by 1995. As car traffic is the major source of NO_x emission, the translation of the national goal for the transportation sector is the reduction of NO_x emission from traffic by at least 30 per cent by 1995. To achieve this goal, catalytic converters have been introduced and were to be obligatory on gasoline engine passenger cars from 1989. A similar measure, to be implemented in 1991, has been approved for buses and trucks. In the larger metropolitan areas, however, especially in the Stockholm area, the extent of the growth of automobile use offsets the positive effects of the introduction of catalytic converters and hence the national goal cannot be met in these areas.

To check the trend in increased automobile use and its adverse environmental effects especially in inner city areas, among the more politically feasible policy measures discussed was an "Area Licensing Scheme", combined with different public transport subsidy levels. Four different policies were evaluated in this context:

1. A decrease in the public transport fare by 50 per cent;
2. An area licensing scheme around the inner city of Stockholm;
3. An area licensing scheme combined with a public transport fare reduction of 50 per cent;
4. An area licensing scheme combined with a public transport fare increase of 50 per cent.

The area licensing scheme would totally surround the inner city of Stockholm, with approximately 30 checkpoints on the cordon line. Because of the geographical location of Stockholm County, the inner city and the road transport network, through traffic would be exempt from toll payment on certain routes. A toll fee of 25 SK per passenger car per round trip was adopted for analysis, the fee level being based on the achievement of environmental goals.

Each of the transport policy measures was evaluated according to the following criteria:

1. The achievement of the national environmental goal of reduction of NO_x emissions by 30 per cent by 1995;
2. Forecasts of NO_x and CO emissions from car traffic in Stockholm County and the inner city area and a partial estimate of the environmental costs of car emission based on NO_x and CO emission;
3. Changes in the travel pattern by car and public transport in Stockholm County and the inner city;
4. Changes in the amount of vehicle kilometres travelled in Stockholm County and in the inner city;
5. Changes in the estimates of travel time by car and public transport and the average speed on the road network;
6. Estimation of public transport revenue and toll revenue.

The analysis of the policy options against the above criteria concluded that two policy measures satisfy the achievement of the national environmental goal. First, an area licensing scheme combined with a public transport fare reduction of 50 per cent adequately achieves the 30 per cent reduction; and second, an area licensing scheme with no change in the public transport fare almost meets this goal. An area licensing scheme combined with a public transport fare reduction of 50 per cent ranked highest in all the other criteria except for that of combined revenues generated from public transport and tolls but it generates enough revenue to finance the public transport network. An area licensing scheme with no change in the public transport fare produces substantially more revenue and if these revenues were allocated to finance the public transport network (as well as the road network), public transport ridership would further increase as the result of the increase in the level of service of public transport.

The proposed scheme has yet to be implemented but the study indicates that substantial environmental and financial benefits can be obtained in transport management if cordon tolls are implemented in appropriate areas and the revenues generated are used to finance the public transport network rather than the road network alone.

Inset 7. *cont'd*

Summary of evaluation of an area licencing scheme as compared with reference scenario 2000

General comments	Increased traffic flow Decreased car polution Decreased public transport subsidy Toll revenue	
	Inner city	Country
Trips		
Car trip	–28%	–6%
Public transport trip	+11%	+5%
Car pollution		
CO	–18%	–10%
NO_x	–18%	–10%
Cost	–248 MSKR/year	
Revenue		
Public transport	+117 MSKR/year	
Toll	+800 MSKR/year	
Total	+917 MSKR/year	

Summary of evaluation of an area licencing scheme combined with a public transport fare reduction of 50% as compared with reference scenario 2 000

General comments	Increased traffic flow Decreased car polution Decreased public transport subsidy Toll revenue	
	Inner city	Country
Trips		
Car trip	–35%	–10%
Public transport trip	+19%	+9%
Car pollution		
CO	–25%	–16%
NO_x	–25%	–16%
Cost	–347 MSKR/year	
Revenue		
Public transport	+665 MSKR/year	
Toll	+717 MSKR/year	
Total	52 MSKR/year	

degree of local support, with only 36.5 per cent of the respondents to a poll in 1986 opposing the toll ring.

Traffic plans

Urban traffic plans are also an effective means of ensuring better co-ordination amongst different transport policies and actions. Various planning measures can be adopted to reduce pollution and nuisance: routing schemes, heavy vehicles bans, speed limits, traffic lights and crossing systems, and pedestrianisation are amongst the many. In Italy, urban traffic plans have recently been implemented to overcome the past inadequacies of unco-ordinated sectoral programmes and projects which disregarded demand for mobility and its implications for land use. Urban traffic plans have the following aims:

1. to rationalise the use of the road network;
2. to rationalise the use of existing parking areas, and to plan new parking areas;
3. to speed up improvements in public and private transport with a view to reduced fuel consumption;
4. to integrate public and private transport systems more closely;
5. to protect the environment in certain areas, even if it means restricting traffic.

In Perugia, such a plan has been used to ease the accessibility and movement in the city centre and preserve the historical nature of the town. The plan consists of an exchange parking system for long stops, whereby cars are prohibited entry into the city centre for long stop periods, and a system of buses moves these people into the city from large parking areas located outside the walls of the historical centre. In addition, a rotating parking system for short stops and mechanised pedestrian routes from these parking facilities have also been implemented. The plan has reduced the number of private vehicles and commercial traffic in the city centre, and the consequent improvement in pollution conditions and general living conditions in the historical centre has led to an increase in citizen and tourist use.

Packaging of measures

A further consideration is that while there is a tendency to treat the various instruments in isolation, there are benefits to be gained by combining a number in one package. The use of differential vehicle taxation in Germany, for example, has hastened the adoption of low emission cars to meet the European emissions norm. In the Stockholm example of cordon pricing, the combination of this policy with subsidised public transport fares will generate significantly greater environmental benefits.

Perhaps one of the most comprehensive projects which "packages" a number of measures to reduce air pollution from traffic is being implemented in Athens, Greece (Inset 8). In 1988 a new Five Year Plan for improving the environmental and social effects of traffic was introduced, creating ring roads around central Athens; establishing new metro lines, extending the trolley bus network and co-ordinating all of the public transport systems; restricting on the movement of traffic in the inner city area; and shifting public service departments out of the inner city and relocating large traffic-related enterprises (e.g. terminals, warehouses) from the centre to entrance points of the Athens basin. This comprehensive policy, however, faces major implementation difficulties and it is important to remember that without effective implementation the packaging of measures will not in itself lead to any environmental benefits.

One of the most forward-looking comprehensive air pollution abatement policies has been proposed in California, United States (Inset 9). Local authorities in the Los Angeles Basin have recently adopted a plan to gradually phase out traditional transport fuels in favour of clean fuels, methanol or electricity. Vehicles in commercial car fleets will gradually be replaced by vehicles running on methanol or electricity. The plan also calls for banning the use of fuel oil and coal in most industrial and utility applications by the mid 1990s so that the only authorised fuels would be natural gas or methanol.

Inset 8. **Packaging of Measures for Air Pollution Abatement from Traffic – The Case of Athens, Greece**

The City of Athens is located in the Athens Basin, which is open to the sea in the south and surrounded by a series of mountains on all other sides. The airshed of the basin has a low ventilation potential during the hot season which lasts for almost eight months of the year and, with the inversion effects created by the surrounding mountains, air pollution concentrates within the basin area. Since 1981, emergency measures have been enacted nine times due to excessive levels of air pollution, the primary cause of which is traffic. In addition to increasing numbers of vehicles, other factors which contribute to the increasing amount of air pollution caused by traffic include: the high average age of cars, which is now 11 years; poor maintenance of vehicles; the use of fuel which contains SO_2 and lead above acceptable levels; the inadequate transport network and the small capacity of public transportation; and the low speed of movement because of congestion which increases emissions.

Building on a previous five year plan (1983-1987) for pollution abatement, which did much for reducing air pollution from industry and central heating, but failed to curb the increasing effects of traffic pollution, a new five-year programme with a multiple package of measures was introduced in 1988. The main characteristics of the programme are:

- The creation of ring roads at various distances around Central Athens, where passenger cars and taxis are permitted to enter every other working day (odd – even number plate system). In days of high levels of air pollution, the area of restricted movement is defined by a larger ring;
- Improvement of fuels (reduction of SO in oil fuel by 30 per cent and in diesel by 40 per cent, reduction of lead in gasoline by 62 per cent);
- Introduction of "cleaner technologies" on all vehicles. Provision of incentives to taxis using petrol to adopt the use of unleaded gasoline;
- Operation of the first Vehicle Control Centres for all buses, taxis and passenger cars and inspection of vehicles;
- The construction of two new metro lines in Central Athens and steps to increase the carrying capacity of the one existing metro line by 20 per cent;
- Extension of the trolley bus network, increasing the numbers of trolley buses and the rearrangement of bus lines with the aim of eliminating terminal stations in Central Athens;
- Computerisation of the traffic lighting system;
- The provision of parking garages along the inner and outer ring, combined with public transport stations;
- A gradual shifting of ministries, public corporations and other public services outside of the Central Business District (CBD);
- Application of varied working hours schedule for public administration and commerce by category of activity; and
- The relocation of establishments of national and regional importance (terminals, warehouses, wholesale) in entrance points of the Athens Basin.

Such comprehensive packages are an effective way of integrating the various aspects that contribute to air pollution caused by traffic in urban areas. Once determined, such programmes need to be efficiently and comprehensively implemented to ensure fulfilment of the desired policy goals. Unfortunately, implementation of the programme in Athens is behind schedule and piecemeal. This low achievement is mostly due to:

- The setting of high performance standards by technical consultants which are in reality beyond what can be reached in Greece;
- Executive agencies which are more concerned with political expediency when managing their investment budgets, than with what is required of them by technical documentation; and
- Lack of continuity among officials responsible for implementing policy due to frequent changes in the Greek political system (ministers and their consultants, governors of public corporations, general secretaries, etc.).

Integrated organisational structures, continuity in responsibility for implementation and appropriate financing are also necessary to ensure the success of policy instruments for ameliorating the urban environment.

Inset 9. **Airshed Quality Management – The Case of Los Angeles, United States**

In early 1989, an extensive three stage programme to improve air quality substantially was adopted for the metropolitan area of Los Angeles, California. The programme's first stage (1989-93) includes tightening restrictions (at a cost of $2.8 billion per year) on the use of private automobiles and on pollution-causing industrial and household activities. During its second stage (1993-98), all diesel buses, 70 per cent of freight vehicles, and 40 per cent of private automobiles will be required to convert to cleaner fuels, with an additional 50 per cent reduction of industrial and consumer-related emissions. The final stage of the programme anticipates the total prohibition of gasoline fuels in automobiles by the year 2007 – a prohibition that assumes the availability of new, as yet unknown, technologies emerging as viable commercial alternatives to gasoline fueled vehicles. A key to the success of the plan is a "redirection" of development patterns, employment and housing locations, and a substantial reduction in travel from homes to employment centres. This "redirection" must be led co-operatively by communities within the Los Angeles metropolitan area.

For especially significant environmental problems, local governments have the ability and the will to take equally significant corrective actions. While a major incentive for local action may be provided through national standards, the actions themselves cannot be taken by the national government alone. The Los Angeles (South Coast Air Quality District) plan is the most drastic, comprehensive and expensive effort to improve air quality ever drawn up locally in the United States. While specific actions proposed were not mandated by the Federal government, court decisions in response to the region's non compliance with Federal air quality standards were a major factor in the development of the local plan. Implementation of the plan will be a local responsibility.

Longer term actions

In the longer term, there is the opportunity for new investment and the introduction of new transport technologies which may be less environmentally intrusive and lead to enhanced economic development. Some of these options involve the replacement of traditional forms of transport by alternative, environmentally-preferable forms (e.g. electronic vehicles) or major changes to the way existing modes are used, but in other cases they represent alternatives to replace current perceptions of transport needs (e.g. telematics and urban design).

While there is often a tendency to treat long and short term strategies as separate issues, they are in fact interrelated. Some short term policies may preclude the adoption of certain longer term actions, while others may set in train a course of action which constrains longer-term changes. Further, given land constraints and inevitable construction delays, new technologies cannot just be suddenly introduced. Initially they must be integrated into the existing transport system and then be gradually expanded to replace it. The actual process of change and the stimulus required to ensure that the changes take due cognizance of environmental matters are, therefore, as important as considering the courses which are open for cities.

Longer term policy options should consider embracing such possibilities as: telematics; urban design; innovative public transport; and computerised automobile control. Some options would seem to be especially advantageous to pursue further as, indeed, the Netherlands' government appears to be doing in the case of high speed vacuum pipeline systems. These offer very rapid forms of subterranean transport, for both persons and goods at low energy costs. Further, since they can be constructed away from existing surface infrastructure and can be complementary to it, they may be more easily developed and deployed than some alternative technologies.

A major consideration in assessing the prospects of cleaner technologies as they are adopted is the cost involved. It is clear, for instance, from the evidence on the current problems of funding urban public transport systems in France, that traditional methods of encouraging the use of less environmentally intrusive modes are not likely to be a viable option for some time, given present policy initiatives. There is a need to tap the private sector for more funding. Transport users need to be made more aware of the current environmental costs they impose by implementing policies which better internalise these social costs of transport use. If appropriate policies for user charges are applied more strictly, for example to automobile use – one of the most environmentally-intrusive forms of urban transport – then this transport medium is likely to become less attractive, which would make other, cleaner technologies a more commercially viable alternative. Taxes imposed on vehicle use rather than on ownership would be a more effective way of internalising the environmental costs of transport.

3. URBAN ENERGY

The issue

Conventional energy sources are limited, but energy remains a commodity with a significant and real potential to be: used more efficiently; supplied from a more flexible, renewable and "unlimited" range of sources; produced with less contribution to environmental degradation; and considered as a service-providing resource rather than a commodity of value entirely unto itself.

Although it is recognised that transport is a significant energy user, the types of strategy necessary for reducing energy demand and environmental degradation from traffic are significantly different from those necessary for managing residential and industrial energy demand in urban areas. This section, therefore, concentrates on strategies for "traditional" urban energy supply and use, whilst the management of transport is dealt with in the previous section.

In global terms, the current practices for the development, conversion and use of energy resources contribute to several problems: global warming; acid rain; health dangers to the population through air pollution and residuals deposition; and depletion of natural resources. These problems already exert significant negative worldwide economic, environmental and social impacts (Table 5). Energy demand and use is therefore a major contributor to the degradation of environmental resources, requiring far-reaching and far-sighted new management strategies if sustainable global development is to occur.

The urban areas of OECD countries are significant users of energy. For example, in the Netherlands, about 35 per cent of national energy consumption is for residential use: 20 per cent for space heating and 15 per cent for lighting (indoor and street lighting) and domestic appliances. In addition, the efficiency of the electrical energy generated for the average Netherlands home is low; only one-third is utilised while two-thirds are lost in generation and distribution. Apart from the waste of energy and raw materials, there are also unnecessary pollution effects. For example, in the United States, between 1970 and 1985, electricity production increased by well over 20 per cent. In the 1982-84 period, electricity accounted for almost half the non-transportation end use energy used in the residential, commercial and industrial sectors. Today, more than five-sixths of all U.S. coal consumption occurs in electric power plants. Two-thirds of all sulphur dioxide emissions and almost one-third of carbon dioxide emissions in the United States result from the operations of coal and oil-fired power plant boilers.

Table 5

IMPORTANCE OF ENERGY ACTIVITIES IN THE GENERATION OF MAJOR POLLUTANTS

Pollutant	Man-made as % of total	Energy activities as % of man-made	Contributions as % of total energy-related releases
SO_2	45%[c]	90%[a]	– Coal combustion: 80%[a] – Oil combustion: 20%[a]
NO_x	75%[c]	85%	– Transport: 51%[a] – Stationary sources: 49%[a]
CO	50%[c]	30-50%[c]	– Transport: 75%[a] – Stationary sources: 25%[a]
Lead	100%[c]	90%[a]	– Transport: 80%[b] – Combustion in stationary sources (including incineration): 20%[b]
PM	11.4%[c]	40%[a]	– Transport: 17%[a] – Electric utilities: 5%[a] – Wood combustion: 12%[a]
VOC	5%[a]	55%[a]	– Oil industry: 15%[a] – Gas industry: 10%[a] – Mobile sources: 75%[a]
Radionuclides	10%[c]	25%[c]	– Mining, milling of uranium: 25%[b] – Nuclear power stations and coal combustion: 75%[b]
CO_2	4%[c]	55-100%[c]	– Natural gas: 19%[b] – Oil: 47%[b] – Coal: 34%[b]
N_2O	25-45%[c]	75-95%[c]	– Fossil fuel combustion: 85%[c] – Biomass burning: 15%[c]
CH4	60%[c]	15-40%[c]	– Natural gas losses: 20-40%[c] – Biomass burning: 30-50%[c]
CFC_3	100%[c]	10-30%[c]	– Refrigeration, air conditioning: 40%[c] – Insulation foam: 60%[c]
Hazardous wastes (excluding nuclear)	100% [c]	12%[b]	– Main sources: combustion of coal and petroleum products, oil refinery, oil drilling and coal mining[d]

a) Estimates for OECD countries.
b) Estimates for United States.
c) Global estimates.
d) Hazardous wastes do not form a homogenous category of pollutants. A percentage breakdown of the contribution of various sources is difficult.

Sources: "Environmental Trends Associated with the 5th National Energy Plan", Argonne National Laboratory, 1986 (for the United States Department of Energy). "A Primer on Greenhouse Gases", D.J. Wuebbles – J. Edmonds, 1988 (for the United States Department of Energy). "The State of the Environment en 1985", OECD, 1985. "The Greenhouse Issue", Environmental Resources Ltd., 1988 (for the Commission of the European Communities).

Cities as major energy users, therefore, need to take new initiatives in the way they manage and use their energy. National and local governments should encourage increased efficiency in energy use, involving increased use of non-polluting energy sources; closed cycle conversion and production processes resulting in increased recycling and decreased waste generation; and decreased use of fossil fuels, with the concurrent development of a series of "multiple" and "renewable" fuel sources.

In the past, energy suppliers at the national, regional and local levels have concentrated on planning for forecasted energy demand by allocating any surplus in present supply and then building new energy generating facilities. Changing economic conditions have made the principal energy source change from oil to hydro-electricity, coal, nuclear and, in some instances, geothermal sources, but it is changing societal attitudes to the state of the local, national and international environment that are causing energy planning to take on a new focus, that of being environmentally friendly. Local energy utilities in many instances are developing new approaches to energy planning for urban areas, along with regional and national efforts. The extent of local initiative is very much a reflection of the extent of control local utilities have over energy resources, a factor which varies substantially between OECD countries.

Sustainable energy use in cities

In the long term, to achieve sustainable energy use it will be necessary to develop global harmonisation of performance standards for urban environment/energy management through policy guidance and continuous information exchange. Such harmonisation will be necessary to ensure that reductions in energy use and associated emissions occur relatively uniformly. In the medium to short term, urban energy management will need to develop strategies to stabilise energy costs, increase energy efficiency and reduce energy emissions to the environment in order to ensure both the economic vitality and social welfare of the community as a whole. For example, cities may significantly aid their prospects for central city revitalisation, business retention and business attraction through conservation, alternative energy sources or preferential utility rates targeted to areas of substantial economic distress.

Cities will require sound methods to evaluate the real relationships between energy efficiency and economic growth, and also to introduce practical management practices to support this relationship. Local governments are in a particularly strong position to define direct linkages between energy management initiatives, their resultant community-wide economic and environmental effects, and practical public/private actions to reduce negative effects. At present a number of innovative approaches are being implemented by cities, often supported by national governments to achieve more efficient energy use and reduce the environmental consequences of energy production.

Innovative approaches

To achieve more sustainable energy use a more comprehensive and integrative management framework will be necessary than has been used in the past. At the city level, a number of different actions to improve the environmental consequences of energy use within urban areas are currently being undertaken. These actions include the use of cleaner technologies, new energy planning strategies, and innovative modelling techniques.

Cleaner or energy saving technologies at supply source

In OECD countries where different energy sources exist, and the local utility has access to ownership, options for the use of more environmentally friendly energy can be implemented. Of greater importance is the ability of local and national authorities to implement cleaner technologies within existing energy sources and combine different energy supply systems in order to generate both cost savings and improvements in the quality of the urban environment. Significant environmental improvement can be gained from the use of cleaner energy sources and the use of technologies that improve environmental quality.

For example, in Finland, Helsinki has undertaken an active programme of implementing cleaner technologies in its power plants and developing power from more environmentally friendly sources. By 1997 all coal-fired power plants will have installed desulphurisation technologies for the control of emissions of smoke gases, which together with the commissioning of a natural gas plant in 1990 will improve the quality of air emissions from energy sources.

Another important technology strategy that has led to significant reduction in energy demand and emissions in several cities has been the implementation of Combined Heat and Power (CHP) plants (Inset 10). In Helsinki, Finland, the city authorities have implemented district heating plants using steam and hot water along with the co-generation of electricity. This system has led to a dramatic decrease of sulphur dioxide in the city's atmosphere and greater fuel utilisation efficiency, with fuel requirements now some 30 per cent less than in a situation where electricity is generated in a condensing power plant and heating is provided by boilers in each building.

Other examples exist in the field of combined "waste burning/heat and power conversion". In Brussels, Belgium, the electricity produced by the burning of municipal waste is equivalent to 130 million KWh per year (Compagnie Générale de Chauffe – Brussels, "Le traitement et la valorisation des déchets"). In Nice, France, 6 000 dwellings and all hospitals are heated by the municipal waste burning plant, which provides two-thirds of the electricity for public consumption in the city. In France, the equivalent of 650 000 TOE per year is produced by municipal waste burning plants, which is mainly used for heating and electricity.

Comprehensive energy planning

Cities faced with an ever increasing demand for energy can no longer depend upon the automatic right to build new urban energy-generating sources. Public concern over efficient resource use and the environmental consequences of different forms of energy have meant that energy planners have had to rethink their supply strategies. One innovative approach to this problem, known as "Least Cost Utility Planning" (LCUP), has been implemented in a number of cities in the United States. LCUP for electricity supplies is a concept that allows the consideration of investments for energy conservation and demand management on an equal footing with investments for new generating capacity. It formally treats energy conservation as an alternative energy source, and will support assessments of non-conventional decentralised smaller generators to substitute for large central generating plants. Applications of this concept require close co-ordination among utility regulators, individual utilities and local governments. To ensure effectiveness, LCUP programmes commonly combine technical support and financial incentives for energy efficiency improvements that are targeted to residential, commercial and industrial consumers. As one example of the

Inset 10. The Role of Combined Heat and Power (CHP) in Energy Conservation and Emission Reduction – The Case of Denmark

In recent decades, Denmark has undertaken a number of technology strategies for energy sectors. The result of these initiatives is that, in the period from 1975 to 1987, the total primary energy requirement for the heating sector in Denmark decreased from 281 TJ/year to 249 TJ/year, despite an increase in the building floor areas from 270 to 325 million m^2. The improvement in the overall energy efficiency of the supply system by expanding the use of Combined Heat and Power/District Heating (CHP/DH) schemes has contributed substantially to this result.

Today, 46 per cent of Denmark's heating requirements are met by district heating and 27 per cent by CHP. Projected extensions of large CHP supply systems and the establishment of 450 Mw decentralised CHP plants will increase CHP coverage to almost 37 per cent of the total heating requirements before the turn of the century. A major reason for the development of CHP/DH systems lies in the technologically more efficient conversion of primary resources into usable final energy forms, heat and electricity, than can be achieved by the separate production of equivalent amounts of the same final energy forms using conventional technology. Fuel inputs are saved and operational costs are lowered.

The latest figures for the conversion efficiency of a conventional steam thermal power plant for electricity production shows that just 40 per cent of the thermal energy input appears as electricity output. The rest is dissipated as heat. It is the partial exploitation of this dissipated energy that facilitates the efficiency enhancements available through the use of CHP. Conversion efficiencies in a CHP plant can be over 80 per cent of the energy input. The gain in conversion efficiency from CHP compared to separate heat and electricity production can range as high as 44 per cent, but may be lower depending upon the application and the power-to-heat ratio proposed. Technical performance and economic attractiveness can vary widely. CHP is viable where a heat load can be exploited, additional to any electricity load that may exist, or vice versa.

One of the additional effects of the energy conservation by using CHP is the reduction of emissions. The local emissions of pollutants, including CO_2, from individual heating plants, are reduced in part from the fuel savings obtained in the CHP process. In addition, the possibility of installing effective emission control equipment is both much greater and much cheaper per produced energy unit in connection with the construction of power plants than in connection with a multiplicity of individual sources.

A comparison of the emission of CO_2 per consumed heat unit from individual sources with the corresponding emission from CHP sources shows that only approximately 30 per cent of the CO_2 emission from individual sources is emitted from CHP plants (Kg CO_2 per TJ).

	Individual	CHP	Reduction %
Coal	146	42	71
Heavy fuel	99	31	69
Natural gas	63	21	67

In order to exemplify the consequences of the CHP development on the environment, the effects of the implementation of the planned CHP supply schemes in Denmark in the year 2000 can be compared with another scenario where the importance of CHP production is limited to a level corresponding to the situation in 1980.

The result of the calculations shows that the planned extension of CHP production will contribute to the following reductions of the emission of CO_2 in the year 2000 compared with a situation without CHP (million tonnes):

	Without CHP	With CHP	Reduction
Coal	+5.18	0.58	4.60
Fuel oil	4.55	0.58	3.97
Natural gas	3.91	0.58	3.32

Environmental questions have until now played a minor role in connection with discussions of the role of combined heat and power. Nonetheless, the energy conservation obtained through a CHP process leads to an evident reduction of the emission of CO_2.

potential of this concept, a utility in the state of Wisconsin avoided new generating facility capital costs of about $500 million by investing $73 million in demand management programmes projected to reduce systemwide demand by 250 Mw by the end of 1990.

Movements to implement principles of least cost planning are in process in the majority of U.S. state utility regulatory commissions. Although there is wide recognition of the potential benefits of LCUP, full adoption of the concept is controversial. For the vast majority of U.S. electric utilities, conservation is not a "profit making" endeavour. Further, significant questions remain concerning the long term stability of conservation "sources", the reliability of small generators, and the equity of cost treatment for all classes of electric consumers. Major efforts to define utility incentives for LCUP and to address questions of stability, reliability and equity are currently in progress.

Having stated the need for an integrated approach, which is the basis of "Least-Cost Utility Planning", it is worthwhile looking at conservation and load management strategies separately (Inset 11).

Conservation strategies

Energy conservation should be an explicit objective in urban design. Conservation strategies can be targeted at the residential, commercial and industrial sectors. Areas of large energy savings include lighting, heating, ventilating and air conditioning systems. In the residential area, Seattle, United States, for example, provides free home weatherisation inspections and advice, plus low interest loans for weatherisation. The city has also developed a list of qualified weatherisation contractors who are authorised to do the work and to be paid from the low interest loans. Encouragement to participate in cost-effective conservation efforts is also provided to self-motivated customers through city-sponsored educational and pilot programmes. These schemes are widespread throughout OECD countries along with programmes for home insulation. A recent study in the northwest of the United Kingdom has shown that, in the domestic sector, even after allowing for increases in comfort levels, the realistic savings potential from well established simple technologies such as cavity wall insulation, draught stripping and improved heating controls is estimated to be 408 000 TOE (162 million therms) p.a. This would be worth £100 million p.a. to householders in the northwest.

In the commercial and industrial areas, Seattle expects to derive large energy savings from conservation. Research and pilot programmes are under way in conjunction with small private industrial plants to build energy conservation into their manufacturing equipment and processes. Several industrial firms have participated in pilot projects to retrofit for energy efficiencies, and then monitor such equipment as motor drives, heating and cooling systems and lighting. In the northwest of the United Kingdom, it has been estimated that in the industrial and commercial sectors there is scope to save 15 per cent of final energy demand from measures using existing technology and with paybacks of two years or less. It is estimated that this could be worth some £250 million p.a. in the region.

With respect to energy saving in the industrial and commercial sectors, an innovative methodology and model has been developed in Berlin, Germany. The model allows for policy-oriented processing of data on energy-related and non-energy-related pollution for a model area of investigation and enables policy advisers, for the first time, to quantify paths of environmental impairment from the emitters at the origin through processes of transmission on to the affected area uses. The application of the model in Berlin has shown that the share of energy-related emissions is high compared to non-energy-related. With respect to

Inset 11. **Least-Cost Utility Planning – The Case of Seattle, United States**

The City of Seattle is located on Puget Sound, Washington State, and is the largest economic centre in the northwest United States. It has a population of almost 500 000 people and inexpensive electric power is a major contributor to both the economic development and quality of life of Seattle. Seattle relies on hydro facilities for most of its power, whether from its own facilities – Seattle City Light (SCL) – or from contracts with the Federal government and other facilities. Much of the impetus for the City to develop its own facilities stems from its partial reliance on purchases of Federal power (approximately 16 per cent) and uncertainty about its future cost.

The OPEC crisis in 1973 and the environmental impacts of building large scale hydroelectric dams saw the end of the hydro power surplus and in 1976, a regional power authority in the northwest United States issued a notice that it could not guarantee supplies of electricity that were sufficient to support Seattle and its region's demands through the next decade. To increase generating capacity, the Authority requested Seattle's financial participation in the construction of two new nuclear generating facilities. Citizens in Seattle expressed strong concern about the necessity of such participation – pressuring the city and its utility to look at alternative means to satisfy its needs.

Seattle responded to this situation with the conduct of a major study to define alternatives. This study called "Energy 1990" included sophisticated load forecasts based on economic models and defining a menu of (non-generating) alternatives to serve future load growth. Results from this first "Least-Cost" planning study in the region recommended a strong emphasis on conservation and indicated that future loads could be met without participation and substantial investment in the development of the two new generating plants. Of perhaps greater importance, the study also began a continuing programme in Seattle that applies "Strategic" planning principles to guide cost-effective and environmentally-sensitive electric power provision. Seattle has established by City Council Resolution the following acquisition goals:

1. Reducing the need to expand or develop new generating facilities through means such as cost-effective conservation;
2. Reducing or containing the costs of producing power through efficiency improvements such as upgrading generator components in dams and other facility improvements that may allow for greater power production at a reduced cost;
3. Providing electricity at the least possible cost by considering all types of generation, or through transmission arrangements with other utilities involving the movement of lower cost electricity to displace higher cost electricity.

Recommended strategy, 1988-2010

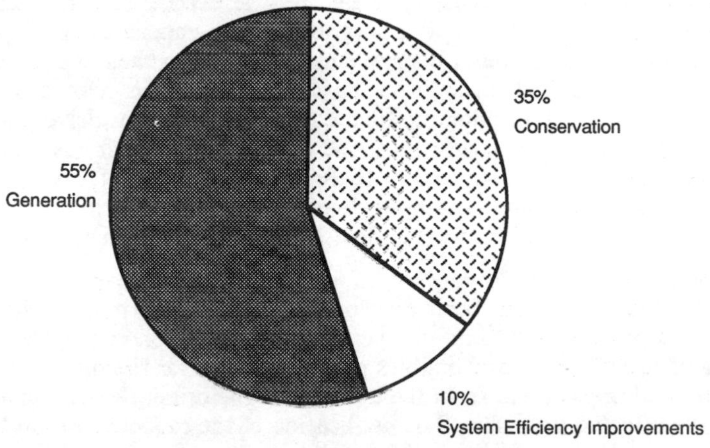

Inset 11. *cont'd*

With leadership from Seattle's Mayor, Council and citizen committees, the city and its municipally-owned utility now produce a biennial Strategic Corporate Plan to guide future electricity provision and resource development actions. The general resource strategy followed in this plan has five major objectives to meet future growth:

1. increase system efficiency;
2. acquire additional conservation resources;
3. acquire medium size hydroelectric facilities;
4. develop cogeneration resources; and
5. increase seasonal interchange with the State of California. New large thermal plants do not appear to play a significant role in Seattle's electric energy future.

With substantial community involvement and sound local leadership, this planning process has proven very successful in balancing both public and private objectives to encourage economic growth, to maintain a stable low cost-energy supply, and do do both in an environmentally-responsible manner.

gaseous air pollutants and dustlike air pollutants, energy-related emissions represent 96 and 77 per cent of the totals respectively. With respect to waste heat, they represent a full 100 per cent, and contribute to 54 per cent of noise pollution. Interestingly, with respect to solid waste and waste water, it was found that non-energy-related emissions were the largest offenders. The model enables energy policy measures to be specifically targeted to individual industries or groups of industry depending upon the geographical location, the type of problem and the available time span, thereby ensuring the efficient implementation and correct targeting of projects to improve energy efficiency and environmental performance (Inset 12).

Performance contracting

Performance contracting is an activity whereby a private investor invests capital and expertise in an energy intensive enterprise so as to bring about energy savings. The investor undertakes to audit, design, install and operate a series of energy conserving activities in return for a share of the company's profits over a defined payback period. The investor, normally a financier, bank or engineer, guarantees the purchaser that their activities will save a certain percentage of a negotiated base line energy use, maintains a positive cash flow for the purchaser of the services and assumes all risks for the proper operation of the improvements. In return, the investor is paid back over a negotiated period of years (typically six to eight) by sharing in the company's savings. The contracts normally have a buy-out clause and at the end of the agreement, the equipment and improvements normally go to the purchaser.

Performance contracting is, therefore, characterised by:

- No capital cost to the purchaser;
- A performance guarantee with all risks assumed by the investor;
- A multi-year term contract with a buy-out provision.

It always results in a neutral cash flow condition and normally a positive cash flow for the purchaser; it encourages private sector R&D in energy saving technologies and improves the uptake of innovations.

Inset 12. **Environmental Improvement Model – Berlin, Germany**

High environmental impairment constitutes an essential barrier to the development of old conurbations. It is well known that the conversion of energy contributes significantly to this pollution problem.

The future living potential of such conurbations as Berlin depends crucially upon a reduction of impairment factors like noise, air pollutants, soil contamination and water pollution. In this way, the use of areas and the possibilities for new industrial settlements in city areas may be improved. This requires more information on the relationship between energy conversion on paths of pollutants and their local and regional impacts. In Berlin, a model has been developed for a policy-oriented way of processing data or energy-related and non-energy-related environmental pollution for an area of investigation. The model makes it possible for the first time to quantify paths of environmental impairment from the emitters at the origin through processes of transmission on to the affected area uses. The model allows for the systematic assessment of the ambiental impairment characteristics of multi-function inner city areas as well as the identification of policy measures.

Elaboration of the model follows five consecutive stages. The first stage is devoted to a systematic assessment of the ambiental impairment characteristics of Berlin. In the second stage, the major paths of pollutants in the area of investigation are identified and described in detail. The third stage quantifies the dispersion of single pollutants from the various emissions into the different environmental media. In the fourth stage, the actual environmental impairments are compared with ambient environmental quality standards and other reference standards. This procedure allows for an evaluation of the toxicity or/and the level of hazardousness. In this stage, the various types of local environmental impairment are also superimposed on each other. This allows for the identification of the most severely polluted areas. In the fifth stage, priorities for policy measures are designed from combining the evaluation and superposition results.

Five stage flow-chart of the local environmental improvement model

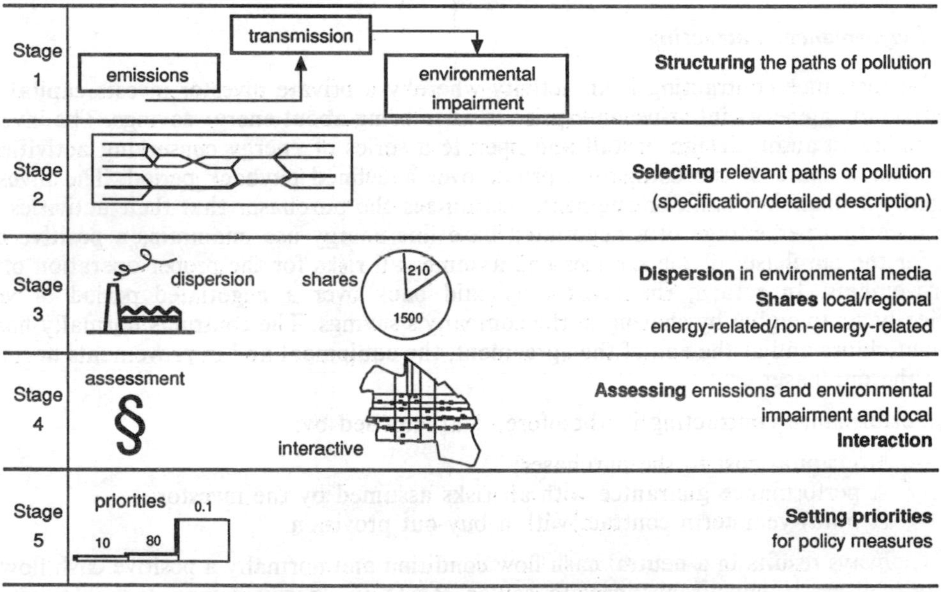

Inset 12. *cont'd*

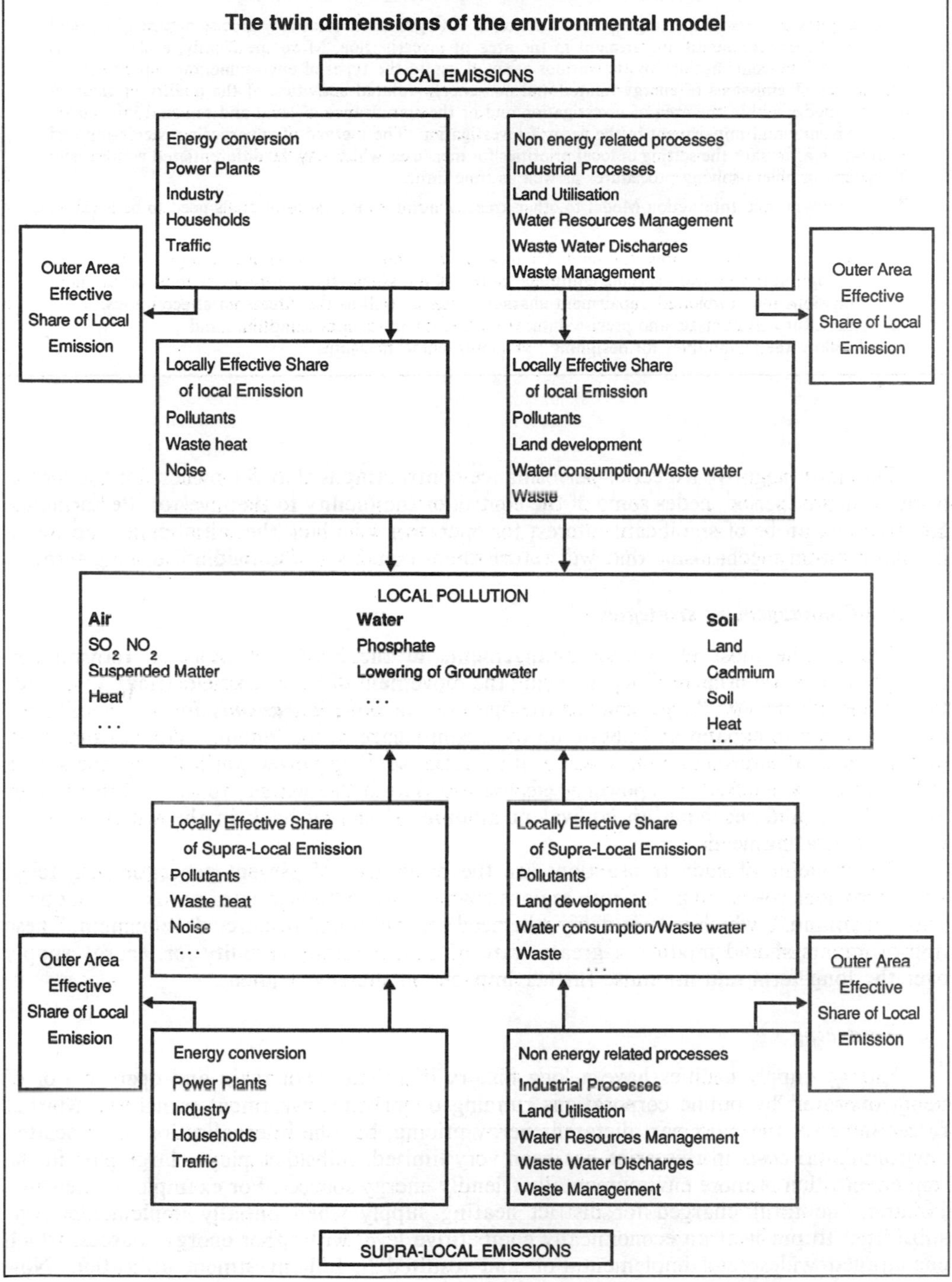

Inset 12. *cont'd*

The complex analysis of the single paths of pollution emerges into a relatively precise picture of the real state of the environmental impairment in the area of investigation. More specifically, a clear view is obtained of the contributions by the various areas of use to the types of environmental impairment, of the shares of emissions of energy-related and non-energy-related activities, of the quality of environmental media within the area of investigation and of the significance of local and regional impacts on the environmental impairment in the area of investigation. The method of superposing, weighting and evaluating allows for the setting of local priorities for measures which may be differentiated with respect to specific problem-solving procedures as well as time limits.

When applying the Interaction Model to other areas, a number of important goals need to be borne in mind:

1. Make a systematic representation of the local environmental conditions, including the interaction among interfering uses, specific emittents, causes of emissions, the conditions of transformation of emissions into ambiental impairment characteristics as well as the effects on affected uses;
2. Work for a systematic and precise data set on the environmental condition; and
3. Explore the possibilities for designing problem-oriented measures.

The main negative aspect of performance contracting is that the owner, for the length of the contract period, cedes some of the control of the facility to the investor. Performance contracting can be of significant interest for operators who lack the initial capital to invest in conservation mechanisms that will return them benefits in the medium to long term.

Load management strategies

One of the most innovative arrangements in the Seattle strategy is transmission arrangements with other utilities involving the movement of lower cost electricity to replace higher cost electricity. At present Seattle operates an ***intertie transmission*** with California and is looking to expand and obtain an ownership share in this facility. This arrangement allows seasonal interchange of power, with Seattle sending power south during the spring and summer (when Seattle's power needs are less than in the winter) to run California's air conditioners, and receiving an equivalent amount of energy back in the winter to meet increased heating needs.

The benefits of such transactions are the better use of present generation capacity, which provides cost savings for both regions (by not having to buy extra power to meet peak season demands), which in turn delays the need for additional resource development. These improvements should produce a greater rate of, and planning stability for, energy supply over the long term and minimise further impacts on the environment.

Financing

Energy supply utilities have a long history of private ownership and operation or of being operated by public corporations running on private investment principles. Market forces have for the most part dictated energy pricing, but the internalisation of associated environmental costs in this price has been very limited. Subsidies play a large part in the implementation of more environmentally friendly energy sources. For example, in Helsinki, Finland, the tariff charged for district heating supply when initially implemented was subsidised to put it at an economically competitive level with other energy sources, which encouraged widespread implementation and resulted in full investment utilisation. Now that economies of scale have been created for this system, any further expansion of the system could be based on recovering the full market cost. Similar strategies are used for introducing scrubbers in coal fired generation plants and for the implementation of conservation projects. Where social benefits in the long term are to be gained from more environmentally sound energy practices, subsidies may be necessary to bring about acceptance, but once established market forces should play a greater role in policy implementation.

FUTURE DIRECTIONS

With the urban environment so high on the policy agenda for the 1990s in so many OECD countries, this report has aimed to provide a timely starting point in establishing new policy guidelines within which urban policy makers can frame individual policy initiatives and also specific projects. This said, this report is essentially exploratory in nature, highlighting some general principles for urban environmental policies by drawing on the diverse experience of Member countries.

The broad themes which emerge here will be further elaborated upon, drawing more extensively on the experiences of individual urban areas. More specifically, further international comparative assessments will be undertaken:

1. ***The relationship of cities to sustainable development*** will be assessed in order to develop further our understanding of the ecosystems of urban areas and how these inter-relate with the global environment. This holistic sectoral and geographical approach will need to be especially concerned with identifying inter-connections and pathways for how cities can contribute to solving global environmental concerns;

2. ***Information on exemplary initiatives and good local practice*** in improving the urban environment and contributing to sustainable global development will be identified and disseminated. This will be based on an evaluation of local initiatives and individual projects, studying all stages of the policy process, through to final considerations such as organisational and financial arrangements, as well as results expressed in quantitative terms;

3. ***Co-operative arrangements between local authorities, the private sector and individuals*** will be examined with a view to improving the capacities of cities to initiate and engage in work beneficial to the environment at local, national and international levels.

These assessments will be undertaken within the new OECD Urban Programme starting in 1991. They will focus on two subjects which have been highlighted as key priorities: "urban travel and sustainable development" and "environmental improvement through urban energy management".

WHERE TO OBTAIN OECD PUBLICATIONS – OÙ OBTENIR LES PUBLICATIONS DE L'OCDE

Argentina – Argentine
Carlos Hirsch S.R.L.
Galería Güemes, Florida 165, 4° Piso
1333 Buenos Aires Tel. 30.7122, 331.1787 y 331.2391
Telegram: Hirsch–Baires
Telex: 21112 UAPE–AR. Ref. s/2901
Telefax:(1)331–1787

Australia – Australie
D.A. Book (Aust.) Pty. Ltd.
648 Whitehorse Road, P.O.B 163
Mitcham, Victoria 3132 Tel. (03)873.4411
Telex: AA37911 DA BOOK
Telefax: (03)873.5679

Austria – Autriche
OECD Publications and Information Centre
4 Simrockstrasse
5300 Bonn (Germany) Tel. (0228)21.60.45
Telex: 8 86300 Bonn
Telefax: (0228)26.11.04

Gerold & Co.
Graben 31
Wien I Tel. (0222)533.50.14

Belgium – Belgique
Jean De Lannoy
Avenue du Roi 202
B–1060 Bruxelles Tel. (02)538.51.69/538.08.41
Telex: 63220 Telefax: (02) 538.08.41

Canada
Renouf Publishing Company Ltd.
1294 Algoma Road
Ottawa, ON K1B 3W8 Tel. (613)741.4333
Telex: 053–4783 Telefax: (613)741.5439
Stores:
61 Sparks Street
Ottawa, ON K1P 5R1 Tel. (613)238.8985
211 Yonge Street
Toronto, ON M5B 1M4 Tel. (416)363.3171

Federal Publications
165 University Avenue
Toronto, ON M5H 3B8 Tel. (416)581.1552
Telefax: (416)581.1743

Les Publications Fédérales
1185 rue de l'Université
Montréal, PQ H3B 3A7 Tel.(514)954–1633

Les Éditions La Liberté Inc.
3020 Chemin Sainte–Foy
Sainte–Foy, PQ G1X 3V6 Tel. (418)658.3763
Telefax: (418)658.3763

Denmark – Danemark
Munksgaard Export and Subscription Service
35, Nørre Søgade, P.O. Box 2148
DK–1016 København K Tel. (45 33)12.85.70
Telex: 19431 MUNKS DK Telefax: (45 33)12.93.87

Finland – Finlande
Akateeminen Kirjakauppa
Keskuskatu 1, P.O. Box 128
00100 Helsinki Tel. (358 0)12141
Telex: 125080 Telefax: (358 0)121.4441

France
OECD/OCDE
Mail Orders/Commandes par correspondance:
2 rue André–Pascal
75775 Paris Cedex 16 Tel. (1)45.24.82.00
Bookshop/Librairie:
33, rue Octave–Feuillet
75016 Paris Tel. (1)45.24.81.67
(1)45.24.81.81
Telex: 620 160 OCDE
Telefax: (33–1)45.24.85.00

Librairie de l'Université
12a, rue Nazareth
13602 Aix–en–Provence Tel. 42.26.18.08

Germany – Allemagne
OECD Publications and Information Centre
Schedestrasse 7
5300 Bonn 1 Tel. (0228)21.60.45
Telefax: (0228)26.11.04

Greece – Grèce
Librairie Kauffmann
28 rue du Stade
105 64 Athens Tel. 322.21.60
Telex: 218187 LIKA Gr

Hong Kong
Swindon Book Co. Ltd.
13 – 15 Lock Road
Kowloon, Hongkong Tel. 366 80 31
Telex: 50 441 SWIN HX
Telefax: 739 49 75

Iceland – Islande
Mál Mog Menning
Laugavegi 18, Pósthólf 392
121 Reykjavik Tel. 15199/24240

India – Inde
Oxford Book and Stationery Co.
Scindia House
New Delhi 110001 Tel. 331.5896/5308
Telex: 31 61990 AM IN
Telefax: (11)332.5993
17 Park Street
Calcutta 700016 Tel. 240832

Indonesia – Indonésie
Pdii–Lipi
P.O. Box 269/JKSMG/88
Jakarta 12790 Tel. 583467
Telex: 62 875

Ireland – Irlande
TDC Publishers – Library Suppliers
12 North Frederick Street
Dublin 1 Tel. 744835/749677
Telex: 33530 TDCP EI Telefax : 748416

Italy – Italie
Libreria Commissionaria Sansoni
Via Benedetto Fortini, 120/10
Casella Post. 552
50125 Firenze Tel. (055)645415
Telex: 570466 Telefax: (39.55)641257

Via Bartolini 29
20155 Milano Tel. 365083
La diffusione delle pubblicazioni OCSE viene assicurata dalle principali librerie ed anche da:
Editrice e Libreria Herder
Piazza Montecitorio 120
00186 Roma Tel. 679.4628
Telex: NATEL I 621427

Libreria Hoepli
Via Hoepli 5
20121 Milano Tel. 865446
Telex: 31.33.95 Telefax: (39.2)805.2886

Libreria Scientifica
Dott. Lucio de Biasio "Aeiou"
Via Meravigli 16
20123 Milano Tel. 807679
Telefax: 800175

Japan– Japon
OECD Publications and Information Centre
Landic Akasaka Building
2–3–4 Akasaka, Minato–ku
Tokyo 107 Tel. 586.2016
Telefax: (81.3)584.7929

Korea – Corée
Kyobo Book Centre Co. Ltd.
P.O. Box 1658, Kwang Hwa Moon
Seoul Tel. (REP)730.78.91
Telefax: 735.0030

Malaysia/Singapore – Malaisie/Singapour
University of Malaya Co–operative Bookshop Ltd.
P.O. Box 1127, Jalan Pantai Baru 59100
Kuala Lumpur
Malaysia Tel. 756.5000/756.5425
Telefax: 757.3661

Information Publications Pte. Ltd.
Pei–Fu Industrial Building
24 New Industrial Road No. 02–06
Singapore 1953 Tel. 283.1786/283.1798
Telefax: 284.8875

Netherlands – Pays–Bas
SDU Uitgeverij
Christoffel Plantijnstraat 2
Postbus 20014
2500 EA's–Gravenhage Tel. (070 3)78.99.11
Voor bestellingen: Tel. (070 3)78.98.80
Telex: 32486 stdru Telefax: (070 3)47.63.51

New Zealand – Nouvelle–Zélande
Government Printing Office
Customer Services
33 The Esplanade – P.O. Box 38–900
Petone, Wellington
Tel. (04) 685–555 Telefax: (04)685–333

Norway – Norvège
Narvesen Info Center – NIC
Bertrand Narvesens vei 2
P.O. Box 6125 Etterstad
0602 Oslo 6 Tel. (02)57.33.00
Telex: 79668 NIC N Telefax: (02)68.19.01

Pakistan
Mirza Book Agency
65 Shahrah Quaid–E–Azam
Lahore 3 Tel. 66839
Telex: 44886 UBL PK. Attn: MIRZA BK

Portugal
Livraria Portugal
Rua do Carmo 70–74
Apart. 2681
1117 Lisboa Codex Tel. 347.49.82/3/4/5
Telefax: 37 02 64

Singapore/Malaysia – Singapour/Malaisie
See "Malaysia/Singapore – "Voir "Malaisie/Singapour"

Spain – Espagne
Mundi–Prensa Libros S.A.
Castelló 37, Apartado 1223
Madrid 28001 Tel. (91) 431.33.99
Telex: 49370 MPLI Telefax: 575 39 98
Libreria Internacional AEDOS
Consejo de Ciento 391
08009 –Barcelona Tel. (93) 301–86–15
Telefax: (93) 317–01–41

Sweden – Suède
Fritzes Fackboksföretaget
Box 16356, S 103 27 STH
Regeringsgatan 12
DS Stockholm Tel. (08)23.89.00
Telex: 12387 Telefax: (08)20.50.21
Subscription Agency/Abonnements:
Wennergren–Williams AB
Box 30004
104 25 Stockholm Tel. (08)54.12.00
Telex: 19937 Telefax: (08)50.82.86

Switzerland – Suisse
OECD Publications and Information Centre
Schedestrasse 7
5300 Bonn 1 Tel. (0228)21.60.45
Telefax: (0228)26.11.04

Librairie Payot
6 rue Grenus
1211 Genève 11 Tel. (022)731.89.50
Telex: 28356
Subscription Agency – Service des Abonnements
4 place Pépinet – BP 3312
1002 Lausanne Tel. (021)341.33.31
Telefax: (021)341.33.45

Maditec S.A.
Ch. des Palettes 4
1020 Renens/Lausanne Tel. (021)635.08.65
Telefax: (021)635.07.80
United Nations Bookshop/Librairie des Nations–Unies
Palais des Nations
1211 Genève 10 Tel. (022)734.60.11 (ext. 48.72)
Telex: 289696 (Attn: Sales)
Telefax: (022)733.98.79

Taiwan – Formose
Good Faith Worldwide Int'l. Co. Ltd.
9th Floor, No. 118, Sec. 2
Chung Hsiao E. Road
Taipei Tel. 391.7396/391.7397
Telefax: (02) 394.9176

Thailand – Thaïlande
Suksit Siam Co. Ltd.
1715 Rama IV Road, Samyan
Bangkok 5 Tel. 251.1630

Turkey – Turquie
Kültur Yayinlari Is–Türk Ltd. Sti.
Atatürk Bulvari No. 191/Kat. 21
Kavaklidere/Ankara Tel. 25.07.60
Dolmabahce Cad. No. 29
Besiktas/Istanbul Tel. 160.71.88
Telex: 43482B

United Kingdom – Royaume–Uni
HMSO
Gen. enquiries Tel. (071) 873 0011
Postal orders only:
P.O. Box 276, London SW8 5DT
Personal Callers HMSO Bookshop
49 High Holborn, London WC1V 6HB
Telex: 297138 Telefax: 071 873 8463
Branches at: Belfast, Birmingham, Bristol, Edinburgh, Manchester

United States – États–Unis
OECD Publications and Information Centre
2001 L Street N.W., Suite 700
Washington, D.C. 20036–4095 Tel. (202)785.6323
Telefax: (202)785.0350

Venezuela
Libreria del Este
Avda F. Miranda 52, Aptdo. 60337
Edificio Galipán
Caracas 106 Tel. 951.1705/951.2307/951.1297
Telegram: Libreste Caracas

Yugoslavia – Yougoslavie
Jugoslovenska Knjiga
Knez Mihajlova 2, P.O. Box 36
Beograd Tel. 621.992
Telex: 12466 jk bgd

Orders and inquiries from countries where Distributors have not yet been appointed should be sent to: OECD Publications Service, 2 rue André–Pascal, 75775 Paris Cedex 16, France.
Les commandes provenant de pays où l'OCDE n'a pas encore désigné de distributeur devraient être adressées à : OCDE, Service des Publications, 2, rue André–Pascal, 75775 Paris Cedex 16, France.

OECD PUBLICATIONS, 2 rue André-Pascal, 75775 PARIS CEDEX 16
PRINTED IN FRANCE
(97 90 03 1) ISBN 92-64-13435-2 - No. 45361 1990

10/90